POEMS BEFORE & AFTER

Books by Miroslav Holub

POETRY

Selected Poems (Penguin Books, 1967)
Although (Jonathan Cape, 1971)
Notes of a Clay Pigeon (Secker & Warburg, 1977)
On the Contrary and other poems (Bloodaxe Books, 1984)
The Fly (Bloodaxe Books, 1987)
Vanishing Lung Syndrome (Faber & Faber, 1990)
Poems Before & After: Collected English Translations
    (Bloodaxe Books, 1990)

PROSE

The Dimension of the Present Moment (Faber & Faber, 1990)
The Jingle Bell Principle (Bloodaxe Books, 1990)

SCIENCE

Immunology of Nude Mice (CRC Press, Boca Raton, Florida, 1989)

MIROSLAV HOLUB

P O E M S

BEFORE & AFTER

COLLECTED ENGLISH TRANSLATIONS BY

IAN & JARMILA MILNER
EWALD OSERS
GEORGE THEINER

BLOODAXE BOOKS

Acknowledgements

Most of the poems *Before* are reprinted from *The Fly* (Bloodaxe Books, 1987), and most of the poems *After* are reprinted from *On the Contrary and other poems* (Bloodaxe Books, 1984). The translations by George Theiner and Ian Milner first appeared in Miroslav Holub's *Selected Poems* (Penguin Modern European Poets, 1967), and are published here by kind permission of Penguin Books Ltd; George Theiner's translation of 'The Prague of Jan Palach' was first published in *The Times Literary Supplement* on 6 February 1969. The translations by Ian and Jarmila Milner first appeared in *Although* (Jonathan Cape, 1971); their translation of 'Super-Aesop' was published in *Poetry Review*.

The translations by Ewald Osers were first published in *The Fly* and *On the Contrary*. The additional translations not included in those two volumes include one by Stuart Friebert and Dana Hábová taken from *Sagittal Section: Poems New and Selected* by Miroslav Holub (Field Translation Series 3, 1980), and four by David Young and Dana Hábová from *Interferon, or On Theater* (Field Translation Series 7, 1982).

The selection was made by Miroslav Holub from the following books:

21-30   *Denní služba* / Day duty (1958)
31-40   *Achilles a želva* / Achilles and the tortoise (1960)
41-62   *Slabikář* / Primer (1961)
63-76   *Jdi a otevři dvere* / Go and open the door (1962)
77-96   *Tak zvané srdce* / The so-called heart (1963)
97-102 *Zcela nesoustavná zoologie* / Totally unsystematic zoology (1963)
103-108 *Kam teče krev* / Where the blood flows (1963)
109-132 *Ačkoli* / Although (1969)
133-140 *Beton* / Concrete (1970)
143-192 *Naopak* / On the contrary (1982)
193-269 *Interferon, čili o divadle* / Interferon, or On Theatre (1986)

Contents

GO AND OPEN THE DOOR (1961)

THE SO-CALLED HEART (1963)

AFTER

Foreword

Miroslav Holub's first collection was published in Prague in 1958. During the next seven years he produced five volumes of poetry, which all sold out quickly. His was a new voice, speaking to his readers arrestingly in unfamiliar modern accents. Until he was thirty he hadn't written poetry. The Second World War, when he was a conscripted railway worker under the Nazi occupation, had interrupted his medical studies. He was now commencing his career as research immunologist at the Microbiological Institute of the Czechoslovak Academy of Sciences in Prague and later in the Institute for Clinical and Experimental Medicine. He has always taken his scientific work very seriously, claiming more than once that it has primacy of importance for him despite his international repute as poet. He has published 130 scientific papers and three monographs and is well known at international conferences and symposia in his field.

Holub has argued in many articles and interviews that scientific method and poetry-making are basically similar: 'The emotional, aesthetic and existential value is the same...when looking into the microscope and seeing the expected (or at times the unexpected, but meaningful) and when looking at the nascent organism of the poem.' It's not surprising that he felt an affinity for the aesthetic of his fellow doctor-poet William Carlos Williams: 'No ideas but in things.' Commenting on some of Williams's poems in 1963 Holub wrote what was close to his own poetic manifesto at the time: 'The foundation of such poetry is therefore no longer the traditionally lyrical or the magically illogical, but the energy, tension and illumination contained within the fact itself.' The key word is 'illumination': the imagination's insight into what 'things' may mean – in themselves and in relation to other things. From the outset Holub's poetic vision was nothing if not contextual. Neither cell nor man lives alone.

His early poems became widely known to English-speaking readers in the *Selected Poems*, edited with an excellent introduction by A. Alvarez, published in their Modern European Poets series by Penguin Books in 1967. They were usually short poems in shrewdly stressed free verse form, stripped of any verbal fat. The concentration on 'things' was there: the poetry was in the 'illumination'. A classic paradigm is 'In the Microscope':

Here too are dreaming landscapes,
lunar, derelict.
Here too are the masses,
tillers of the soil.
And cells, fighters
who lay down their lives
for a song.

Here too are cemeteries,
fame and snow.
And I hear murmuring,
the revolt of immense estates.

Carlos Williams's red wheelbarrow upon which 'so much depends' stands there, imagistically, 'glazed with rain / water / beside the white / chickens'. Holub's cells are 'fighters / who lay down their lives / for a song' and foreshadow 'the revolt of immense estates'. The image of 'fact' has become the metaphor of imaginative transmutation.

The early poems had, and still vividly retain, another kind of appeal: their ironic and satiric impact. Written against the background of the Stalinist 1950s and a rigorous censorship apparatus, the irony had to be expressed mostly by the indirect means of allegory and fable. Holub made himself a master of poetic double-talk, enlivened by a mordant wit. The pace of democratic change in his country today shouldn't let us forget the stifling pre-1968 atmosphere of which he wrote his so memorable register in 'The Door':

Go and open the door.
    Even if there's only
    the darkness ticking,
    even if there's only
    the hollow wind,
    even if
            nothing
                    is there,
go and open the door.

At least
there'll be
a draught.

Marianne Moore called on the modern poet to present 'imaginary gardens with real toads in them'. (Dr Holub might have said nude mice). In his poetry of the seventies and eighties the 'imaginary gardens' grow more expansive in the stylisation. But the mood is often darker, the irony more bitter, the underlying humanism and trust in reason soured by scepticism. These are the poems of *after* 1968, after the crushing of the democratic revival.

Explaining why he had moved away from the short free verse poem of 'before', Holub told me in an interview: 'It's not the thing said that so much interests me as the way of saying it. I needed a more complicated structure.' One kind of imaginary garden was the 'stage' and puppet poems included in the 'after' part of this book. The whimsically chosen dramatis personae and puppet clowns opened the door to his lively feeling for fantasy, verbal play, and what Ted Hughes once called 'the surrealism of folk-lore'. It was often fantasy in the vein of Beckett and Ionesco: the theatre of the absurd updated and adapted for satiric mockery and demolition of the real and, for so many, tragic absurdities of 'after'.

There is a cutting edge to the satire of some of these 'dramatic' pieces, as in the elaborate and verbally scintillating 'Super-Aesop', 'The Angel of Death', or 'Sand game'. In others one senses the spirit of carnival, of the absurd played to excess for comic relief.

> I'll slip out in front of the curtain, taking
> great care not to tangle my strings
> in the flies,
> I'll jingle my bells (merrily),
> doff my cap
> and before the puppeteer know's what happening
> I'll speak in my own voice,
> you know,
> my own voice,
> out of my own head,
> for the first and the last time,
> because afterwards they'll put me back in the box,
> wrapped in tissue paper.

Punch the puppet is speaking in the poem 'Punch's dream'. Holub is speaking too – for himself and for all the others, whether writers, artists, teachers, doctors, bricklayers, waitresses, or technicians, who were silenced, except for the resolute few, following 1968. He wasn't able to publish in his own country until 1982. Abroad he risked publishing some of the 'after' poems without official sanction. The poetry of this time is utterly without illusions. Or evident grounds for hope. Nor is there cynicism or the cul-de-sac of nothingness. Underlying many of the poems is what Zbigniew Herbert called 'a sense of responsibility, a sense of responsibility for the human conscience'. Although Punch knows that 'they' will put him 'back in the box', he *will* speak in his own voice, out of his own head.

Though many of Holub's best-known poems proceed from response to a specific social and cultural milieu, they aren't circumscribed by it. His poetic range reaches far beyond any possible

15

limits of locale, especially in his later work. An alert ever-curious intelligence, scientific awareness, roving interest in world history and mythology, and philosophic cast of mind combine to make his poetry universally referential. His finest reflective poems, such as 'Suffering', 'The root of the matter' (complex and well constructed), 'On the Origin of 6pm', 'Interferon', 'Whaling', explore, sometimes dissect, the ultimate nerves of being, of human existence in its most exposed aspects, positive and negative.

In these poems of existentialist inquiry the terse skeletal structure of much of the early work is fleshed out with an enriching figurative density and colouring. The tough-grained intelligence is always evident, but is more and more mediated by a mercurial imagination that recreates the intellectual perceptions in arresting metaphor. The poet's 'knowledge passes instantaneously into feeling, and feeling flashes back as a new organ of knowledge', as George Eliot put it. In 'The root of the matter' Holub has his imagined Faust confronting mortality in the form of a poodle senselessly run over by a bus before his eyes. The 'nonplussed' Faust says:

> dog and nothing but a dog, black, white or other,
> empty-handed messenger, because there is no
> mystery
> except the thread which from our hands
> leads round the far side of things, round the collar of the landscape
> and up the sleeve of a star.
> *The root of the matter is not*
> *in the matter itself*

No other poet of our time has more vividly and accurately made his poetry both an existentialist microscope and social barometer. Nor so persuasively shown throughout a thirty-year variegated corpus how the insights of the scientific mind can be sea-changed into poetry of the highest order.

IAN MILNER
Prague, March 1990

BEFORE

DAY DUTY
DENNÍ SLUŽBA
(1958)

Cinderella

Cinderella is sorting her peas:
bad ones those, good ones these,
yes and no, no and yes.
No cheating. No untruthfulness.

From somewhere the sound of dancing.
Somebody's horses are prancing.
Somebody's riding in state.

The slipper's no longer too small,
toes have been cut off for the ball.
This is the truth. Never doubt.

Cinderella is sorting her peas:
bad ones those, good ones these,
yes and no, no and yes.
No cheating. No untruthfulness.

Coaches drive to the palace door
and everybody bows before
the self-appointed bride.

No blood is flowing. Just red birds
from distant parts are clearly heard
as, plumage ruffled, they alight.

Cinderella is sorting her peas:
bad ones those, good ones these,
yes and no, no and yes.

No little nuts, no prince that charms
and we all long for mother's arms,
yet there is but one hope:

Cinderella is sorting her peas:
softly as one fits joints together
with fingers gentle as a feather,
or as one kneads the dough for bread.

And though it may be light as air,
merely a song in someone's head
a gossamer of truth is there.

Cinderella is sorting her peas:
bad ones those, good ones these,
yes and no, no and yes,
no cheating in this bout.

She knows that she is on her own.
No helpful pigeons; she's alone.
And yet the peas, they *will* be sorted out.

[EO]

Graves of prisoners

'Jemand erzählt von seiner Mutter...'
R.M. RILKE

Šumava Mountains; bulls' horns locked
in fight on trampled soil
piled into hill and rock.

Deserted frontier, deathbed-like,
an abandoned house nearby.
Resisting maples strike
out for the sky.

A cemetery, crumbling, grey,
black lilac choking the stone.
What have those wolfish rains washed away?
And what have they left alone?

Below a ruined wall
four graves still tell a story:
Kolisan Alexandr,
Gavril Kondratenko,
Tatshenko Vladimir,
Henri Joly.

Prisoners. In nineteen forty-two.
And still on the graves no grass will grow,
as if thin smoke hung over them,
as if their bodies rose up from below.

As if they were holding hands.

Under the rain-drenched maples it seems
as if a fire were flickering gently,
as if someone were sitting there
and listening intently.

Someone with an accordion
on this damp, unhealed clay.
Picks it up. Starts to play.
Someone speaks of some campaign or other.

Someone speaks of his mother.

[EO]

The flypaper

The kitchen's buzzing conscience:
death of the guilty and innocent,

Sisyphuses.

Behold an earthly paradise
without midge, gnat or fly.

Arbeit macht frei.

[EO]

26

Harbour

But the sea was measured
and chained to the earth.
And the earth was measured
and chained to the sea.

They launched
cranes, lean angels,
they calculated
the wail of widowed sirens,
they foresaw
the nervous unrest of buoys,
they drafted
the labyrinth of routes around the world.

They constructed
the Minotaurs of ships.

They discovered five continents.

The earth was measured
and chained to the sea.
And the sea was measured
and chained to the earth.

All that is left
is a small house above the canal.
A man who spoke softly,
a woman with tears in her eyes.
All that is left is the evening lamp,
the continent of the table,
the tablecloth, a seagull that does not fly away.

All that is left
is a cup of tea,
the deepest ocean in the world.

[GT]

In the microscope

Here too are dreaming landscapes,
lunar, derelict.
Here too are the masses,
tillers of the soil.
And cells, fighters
who lay down their lives
for a song.

Here too are cemeteries,
fame and snow.
And I hear murmuring,
the revolt of immense estates.

[IM]

Pathology

Here in the Lord's bosom rest
the tongues of beggars,
the lungs of generals,
the eyes of informers,
the skins of martyrs,

in the absolute
of the microscope's lenses.

I leaf through Old Testament slices of liver,
in the white monuments of brain I read
the hieroglyphs
of decay.

Behold, Christians,
Heaven, Hell, and Paradise
in bottles.
And no wailing,
not even a sigh.
Only the dust moans.
Dumb is history
strained
through capillaries.

Equality dumb. Fraternity dumb.

And out of the tricolours of mortal suffering
we day after day
pull
threads of wisdom.

[GT]

Casualty

They bring us crushed fingers,
mend it, doctor.
They bring burnt-out eyes,
hounded owls of hearts,
they bring a hundred white bodies,
a hundred red bodies,
a hundred black bodies,
mend it, doctor,
on the dishes of ambulances they bring
the madness of blood
the scream of flesh,
the silence of charring,
mend it, doctor.

And while we are suturing
inch after inch,
night after night,
nerve to nerve,
muscle to muscle,
eyes to sight,
they bring in
even longer daggers,
even more thunderous bombs,
even more glorious victories,

idiots.

[EO]

ACHILLES & THE TORTOISE
ACHILLES A ŽELVA
(1960)

Night in the streets

They are singing
at the bird-fancier's.
The houses are growing.

A few bricks
are coming away from the cathedral.
Here and there
a feather
or a cat
or dog
falls from the sky.

They are singing
at the bird-fancier's.

The houses are growing.
In their walls runs
the white blood of the just.
On the breath of millions
the moon rises,
the immense heart
rolls night towards day.

It's enough that we are alive.
Are breathing.

Responsible
even for the rotation of the earth.

[IM]

Napoleon

Children, when was
Napoleon Bonaparte born,
asks teacher.

A thousand years ago, the children say.
A hundred years ago, the children say.
Last year, the children say.
No one knows.

Children, what did
Napoleon Bonaparte do,
asks teacher.

Won a war, the children say.
Lost a war, the children say.
No one knows.

Our butcher had a dog
called Napoleon,
says František.
The butcher used to beat him and the dog died
of hunger
a year ago.

And all the children are now sorry
for Napoleon.

[IM/JM]

The Corporal who killed Archimedes

With one bold stroke
he killed the circle, tangent
and point of intersection of parallels
in infinity.

On penalty
of quartering
he banned numbers
from three up.

Now in Syracuse
he heads a school of philosophers,
squats on his halberd
for another thousand years
and writes:

one two
one two
one two
one two

[IM/JM]

Death in the evening

High, high.

Her last words wandered across the ceiling
like clouds.
The sideboard wept.
The apron shivered
as if covering an abyss.

The end. The young ones had gone to bed.

But towards midnight
the dead woman got up,
put out the candles (a pity to waste them),
quickly mended the last stocking,
found her fifty nickels
in the cinnamon tin
and put them on the table,
found the scissors fallen behind the cupboard,
found a glove
they had lost a year ago,
tried all the door knobs,
tightened the tap,
finished her coffee,
and fell back again.

In the morning they took her away.
She was cremated.
The ashes were coarse
as coal.

[GT]

Five minutes after the air raid

In Pilsen,
twenty-six Station Road,
she climbed to the third floor
up stairs which were all that was left
of the whole house,
she opened her door
full on to the sky,
stood gaping over the edge.

For this was the place
the world ended.

Then
she locked up carefully
lest someone steal
Sirius
or Aldebaran
from her kitchen,
went back downstairs
and settled herself
to wait
for the house to rise again
and for her husband to rise from the ashes
and for her children's hands and feet to be stuck back in place.

In the morning they found her
still as stone,
sparrows pecking her hands.

[GT]

Explosion

Yes;
but then came
bricklayers,
doctors,
carpenters,
    people with shovels,
    people with hopes,
    people with rags,
stroked
the loins of the wild house,
stroked
the pounding heart of space,
stroked the crest of pain

until all the bricks came back,
until all the drops of blood came back,
all the molecules of oxygen

and stone
pardoned stone.

[IM/JM]

Home I.

From amidst last year's cobwebs
she glanced up from a creaking easy-chair:
'You're looking well, boy.'

And wounds were healing,
we were children again,
and no school today.

And when things were at their worst,
with no night and no day
and no up and no down
and we barely dared breathe,

she'd say
from amidst her cobwebs:
'You're looking well boy.'

And wounds would heal before her eyes
even though she was

blind.

[EO]

Voices in the landscape

The mist stays awake.
From infinite distance comes the howling of lemurs.
The grass's soul laughs happily in the moonlight.
And people think the air is crying.

Darkness gnaws at the trees.

The soul of a legless baker
has a story of yeast to tell.
The strung-up forest
sings in the willow slips.
A seamstress climbs
down the thread from
a tubercular room.

Night oxygenated by eternity.

Soldiers,
tunics still white,
playing the hurdygurdy
of level-crossing gates.

The tavern's roar in tiny pebbles.

At the break of day
the ghosts will die
and be finally laid to rest
in a thimble
in loaves of bread,
in cubic metres,
in thresholds
and in door-handles

everlasting
like us.

[EO]

PRIMER
SLABIKÁŘ
(1961)

Alphabet

Ten million years
from the Miocene
to the primary school in Ječná Street.

We know everything
from *a* to *z*.

But sometimes the finger stops
in that empty space between *a* and *b*,
empty as the prairie at night,

between *g* and *h*,
deep as the eyes of the sea,

between *m* and *n*,
long as man's birth,

sometimes it stops
in the galactic cold
after the letter *z*,
at the beginning and the end,

trembling a little
like some strange bird.

Not from despair.

Just like that.

[EO]

A history lesson

Kings
like golden gleams
made with a mirror on the wall.

A non-alcoholic pope,
knights without arms,
arms without knights.

The dead like so many strained noodles,
a pound of those fallen in battle,
two ounces of those who were executed,

several heads
like so many potatoes
shaken into a cap –

Geniuses conceived
by the mating of dates
are soaked up by the ceiling into infinity

to the sound of tinny thunder,
the rumble of bellies,
shouts of hurrah,

empires rise and fall
at a wave of the pointer,
the blood is blotted out –

And only one small boy,
who was not paying the least attention,
will ask
between two victorious wars:

And did it hurt in those days too?

[GT]

The sick primer

Even the primer
may
fall sick one day
    because
    the children are good and work hard.
    But that isn't really quite true,
    the leaves drop in the autumn,
    but that isn't really quite true,
    flames burn, the moon shines,
    but that isn't really quite true.
    Dad may work his fingers to the bone,
    but that isn't really quite true,
    this is now and that is later,
    but that isn't really quite true,

even the primer
may
fall sick one day with
what isn't really quite true,
the worst
contagious disease,
with paper fevers,
with black-and-white hallucinations,
with superstitious spots,

wise men
will bandage the primer,
cover the primer,
lock up the primer
    (better a half-truth than nothing),

but the primer
will talk
in its sleep,
    don't believe in ghosts,
    don't believe in plaster,
    in eyes or in ears,
    don't believe in words,

the primer
will talk
in its sleep,
> better a temporary nothing
> than definitive half-truths,
it will call out,
> try a bit harder, for Chrissake,
> get your noddles working,
> don't swallow your own lies,

wise men
will sentence the insane primer
for illiteracy,
> to be set to music,
> to be billed as a poster,
> to be translated
> into a dead language,

and children
themselves
will have to paint a dot,
some will paint the sun,
some will draw a circle
with compasses, for an alpha plus,

and the teacher will say
I shall never get through
testing and marking
that lot.

[EO]

Midday

Day has cast anchor in the shallows.

Trees tremble with happiness,
immortal
butterflies sing.

The sky is sweet
as a face we love
that day.

Children's small voices
tumble down the hillsides.

Sun, song, peace:

something's impending.

[EO]

The rain at night

With mouse-like teeth
the rain gnaws at stone.
The trees parade through the town
like prophets.

Perhaps it's the sobbing
of the monstrous angels of darkness,
perhaps the suppressed laughter
of the flowers out there in the garden,
trying to cure consumption
by rustling.

Perhaps the purring
of the holy drought
under any kind of cover.

An unspeakable time,
when the voice of loudspeakers cracks
and poems
are made not of words
but of drops.

[GT]

The forest

Among the primary rocks
where the bird spirits
crack the granite seeds
and the tree statues
with their black arms
threaten the clouds,

suddenly
there comes a rumble,
as if history
were being uprooted,

the grass bristles,
boulders tremble,
the earth's surface cracks

and there grows

a mushroom,

immense as life itself,
filled with billions of cells
immense as life itself,
eternal,
watery,

appearing in this world for the first

and last time.

[GT]

Haul of fish

The court is in session.

And all that is hidden
shall be revealed.

In the last fish-pond
the last fish
on the dried-up bed
soundlessly dies.

And the terror of the gills
and the terror of slime

contentedly

rise to the skies.

[EO]

Spice

A bay leaf from Baghdad,
pepper from Zanzibar,
marjoram from Casablanca.

These are the smell of home.

The cities' houses exactly
as pictures in the album,
hovels on the desert's edge,
yellowing,
like those tins on the sideboard.

The bewitching taste of distant lands.

[EO]

The fly

She sat on a willow-trunk
watching
part of the battle of Crécy,
the shouts,
the gasps,
the groans,
the tramping and the tumbling.

During the fourteenth charge
of the French cavalry
she mated
with a brown-eyed male fly
from Vadincourt.

She rubbed her legs together
as she sat on a disembowelled horse
meditating
on the immortality of flies.

With relief she alighted
on the blue tongue
of the Duke of Clervaux.

When silence settled
and only the whisper of decay
softly circled the bodies

and only
a few arms and legs
still twitched jerkily under the trees,

she began to lay her eggs
on the single eye
of Johann Uhr,
the Royal Armourer.

And thus it was
that she was eaten by a swift
fleeing
from the fires of Estrées.

52

Shooting galleries

All over the place
shooting galleries arrive,
boys are getting ready
to hunt
tin clowns.

At night
the rifles grind their teeth,
paper roses smell sweet on the graves
of the peeling fallen.

All over the place
shooting galleries leave,
and in trampled grass
a scarlet
drop of blood
remains.

[EO]

Textbook of a dead language

This is a boy.
This is a girl.

The boy has a dog.
The girl has a cat.

What colour is the dog?
What colour is the cat?

The boy and the girl
are playing with a ball.

Where is the ball rolling?

Where is the boy buried?
Where is the girl buried?

Read
and translate
into every silence and every language!

Write
where you yourselves
are buried!

[GT]

54

The village green

The memorial of our heroes
has crumbled into stone:
the last casualty of the last war.

The sky over that spot
is healing the scar,
the goose fanfare
calls the wounded sward back to life.

But under the ground a mouse
says to another,
about to give birth:
Not here, come a bit farther!

[GT]

Polonius

Behind every arras
he does his duty
unswervingly.
Walls are his ears,
keyholes his eyes.

He slinks up the stairs,
oozes from the ceiling,
floats through the door
ready to give evidence,
prove what is proven,
stab with a needle
or pin on an order.

His poems always rhyme,
his brush is dipped in honey,
his music flutes
from marzipan and cane.

You buy him
by weight, boneless,
a pound of wax flesh,
a pound of mousy philosophy,
a pound of jellied
flunkey.

And when he's sold out
and the left-overs wrapped
in a tasselled obituary,
a paranoid funeral notice,

and when the spore-creating mould
of memory
covers him over,
when he falls
arse-first to the stars,

the whole continent will be lighter,
earth's axis straighten up
and in night's thunderous arena
a bird will chirp in gratitude.

[IM]

Love

Two thousand cigarettes.
A hundred miles
from wall to wall.
An eternity and a half of vigils
blanker than snow.

Tons of words
old as the tracks
of a platypus in the sand.

A hundred books we didn't write.
A hundred pyramids we didn't build.

Sweepings.
Dust.

Bitter
as the beginning of the world.

Believe me when I say
it was beautiful.

[IM]

Bones

We lay aside
   useless bones,
   ribs of reptiles,
   jawbones of cats,
   the hip-bone of the storm,
   the wish-bone of Fate.

   To prop the growing head
   of Man
We seek
   a backbone
   that will stay
   straight.

[GT]

The geology of man

Some
natural common
cause.

Some
elementary value
of life.

Some goodness
of heart
or liver
or whatever.

These depths are in the sand.

It only takes
a bad storm,
a dash of alcohol,
a drop of grandmother's.
superstition

and the flood is here.

Goodness
is orogeny.

Without a magnetic
overburden of necessity
not a hair of sense
is etched.

Only continuous
internal bleeding
coagulating in the fissures
into basalts and granites.

Man
is just drudgery
for two million years.

[EO]

Wings

We have
microscopic anatomy
of the whale
this
is
reassuring
    WILLIAM CARLOS WILLIAMS

We have
a map of the universe
for microbes,
we have
a map of a microbe
for the universe.

We have
a Grand Master of chess
made of electronic circuits.

But above all
we have
the ability
to sort peas,
to cup water in our hands,
to seek
the right screw
under the sofa
for hours

This
gives us
wings.

[GT]

A helping hand

We gave a helping hand to grass –
  and it turned into corn.
We gave a helping hand to fire –
  and it turned into a rocket.
Hesitatingly,
cautiously,
we give a helping hand
to people,
to some people...

[GT]

Ode to joy

You only love
when you love in vain.

Try another radio probe
when ten have failed,
take two hundred rabbits
when a hundred have died:
only this is science.

You ask the secret.
It has just one name:
again.

In the end
a dog carries in his jaws
his image in the water,
people rivet the new moon,
I love you.

Like caryatids
our lifted arms
hold up time's granite load

and defeated
we shall always win.

[IM]

GO AND OPEN THE DOOR
JDI A OTEVŘI DVERE
(1962)

The door

Go and open the door.
  Maybe outside there's
  a tree, or a wood,
  a garden,
  or a magic city.

Go and open the door.
  Maybe a dog's rummaging.
  Maybe you'll see a face,
or an eye,
or the picture
              of a picture.

Go and open the door.
  If there's a fog
  it will clear.

Go and open the door.
  Even if there's only
  the darkness ticking,
  even if there's only
  the hollow wind,
  even if
          nothing
                  is there,
go and open the door.

At least
there'll be
a draught.

[IM]

64

Evening idyll with a protoplasm

Over the houses spreads
the eczema of twilight,
the evening news bulletin
creeps across the façades,
the beefburger is singing.

A protoplasm called
well-that's-life
bulges from all the windows,
tentacles with sharp-eyed old hags' heads,
it engulfs a pedestrian,
penetrates into beds across the road,
swallowing tears and fragments of quarrels,
pregnancies and miscarriages,
splashing used cars and television sets,
playing havoc with the price of eggs,
slimily puffing itself with adulteries,
crossing off plotting spores of
things-were-different-in-our-day.

And even after dark it phosphoresces
like a dead sea drying up

between featherbed, plum jam and stratosphere.

[EO]

A few very clever people

Their words were pins,
their silences needles.

Night with cold hands
was leaning on
the unstitched animal of the world.

And walking home
they kicked
         a loaf
from one corner
            to the next.

[EO]

The teacher

The earth rotates,
             says the young pupil.
Not so, the earth rotates,
             says the teacher.

The hills are turning green,
             says the young pupil.
Not so, the hills are turning green,
             says the teacher.

Twice two is four,
             says the young pupil.
Not so, twice two is four,
             the teacher corrects him.

Because the teacher knows best.

[EO]

67

The best room, or interpretation of a poem

And now tell it to me
in other words,
says the stuffed owl
to the fly
which, with a buzz,
is trying with its head
to break through the window-pane.

[EO]

Žito the magician

To amuse His Royal Majesty he will change water into wine.
Frogs into footmen. Beetles into bailiffs. And make a Minister
out of a rat. He bows, and daisies grow from his finger-tips.
And a talking bird sits on his shoulder.

There.

Think up something else, demands His Royal Majesty.
Think up a black star. So he thinks up a black star.
Think up dry water. So he thinks up dry water.
Think up a river bound with straw-bands. So he does.

There.

Then along comes a student and asks: Think up sine alpha
greater than one.

And Žito grows pale and sad: Terribly sorry. Sine is
between plus one and minus one. Nothing you can do about that.
And he leaves the great royal empire, quietly weaves his way
through the throng of courtiers, to his home
                                    in a nutshell.

[GT]

Inventions

Wise men in long white togas come forward during the
festivities, rendering account of their labours,
and King Belos listens.

O, mighty King, says the first, I've made a pair of wings
for your throne. You shall rule from the air. –
Then applause and cheering follow, the man is
richly rewarded.

O, mighty King, says the second, I've made a self-acting
dragon which will automatically defeat your foes. –
Then applause and cheering follow, the man is
richly rewarded.

O, mighty King, says the third, I've made a destroyer
of bad dreams. Now nothing shall disturb your royal sleep. –
Then applause and cheering follow, the man is
richly rewarded.

But the fourth man only says: Constant failure has dogged
my steps this year. Nothing went right. I bungled everything
I touched. – Horrified silence follows and
the wise King Belos is silent too.

It was ascertained later that the fourth man was
Archimedes.

[GT]

Merry-go-round

Some ride on chestnut mares
to plum-jam Argentina,
some ride in atomic trams
into space
without holding on.

The music oozes from the lowering sky
like the past century
wailing overhead
for all we used to love
and will love yet.

And the riders on horseback
and the red tram's passengers
will be
       aviators
            and engineèrs.

But the little boy who
crouches to watch the electric motor below,
the electric motor driving the noontide witch,
the gingerbread cottages
and the sclerotic
cardboard princess,

the little boy
who remarked –
why, this thing runs as smooth as shit –
that little boy
will be a poet.

[EO]

Poem technology

It is
   a fuse,
you light
somewhere in the grass,
or in a cave,
or in a third-rate
                  saloon.

The little flame races
among the blades,
among the startled butterflies,
among terrified stones, among sleepy tankards,
racing,

growing a little or vanishing
like pain in a supernumerary finger,
hissing, spluttering,
halting
      in microscopic vertigo,

but right at the end
                  it explodes,
a boom as from a cannon,
tatters of words fly through the universe,
the day's walls reverberate,

but even if
no rock is burst
someone will say at least –
            Hell, something's happened!

[EO]

72

The bell

In this house no one has a bell. Everyone
recognises his visitors through the wall,
if any come at all.

Only the oldest woman, a lady lonely as a rat, had
a shrilly-tuned bell
fixed to her doorpost,
so it could stay silent year
after year.
Yet one day on the stairs there'll be a white
unicorn and he will ring without expecting an answer.

And the old lady will open her door and call
after him:
Thank you, unicorn!

[EO]

A dog in the quarry

The day was so bright
  that even birdcages flew open.
The breasts of lawns
  heaved with joy
and the cars on the highway
  sang the great song of asphalt.
At Lobzy a dog fell in the quarry
  and howled.
Mothers pushed their prams out of the park opposite
because babies cannot sleep
  when a dog howls,
and a fat old pensioner was cursing the Municipality:
they let the dog fall in the quarry and then leave him there,
and this, if you please, has been going on since morning.

Towards evening even the trees
  stopped blossoming
and the water at the bottom of the quarry
  grew green with death.
But still the dog howled.

Then along came some boys
and made a raft out of two logs
and two planks.
And a man left on the bank
a briefcase, in which bread is planted
  in the morning
so that by noon
  crumbs may sprout in it
(the kind of briefcase in which documents
  and deeds
  would die of cramp),
he laid aside his briefcase
and sailed with them.

Their way led across a green puddle
to the island where the dog waited.
It was a voyage like
  the discovery of America,

a voyage like
   the quest of Theseus.
The dog fell silent,
   the boys stood like statues
and one of them punted with a stick,
the waves shimmered nervously,
tadpoles swiftly
   flickered out of the wake,
the heavens
   stood still,
and the man stretched out his hand.

It was a hand
   reaching out across the ages,
it was a hand
   linking
   one world with another,
   life with death,
it was a hand
   joining everything together,
it caught the dog by the scruff of its neck

and then they sailed back
to the music of
an immense fanfare
of the dog's yapping.

It was not a question of that one dog.

It was not a question of that park.

Somehow it was a question
of our whole childhood,
   all of whose mischiefs
   will eventually out,
of all our loves,
of all the places we loved in
   and parted never to meet again,
of every prospect
   happy as grass,
unhappy as bone,
of every path up or down,

of every raft and all the other machines
we search for at our lathes
    and drawing-boards,
of everything we are reaching out for
round the corner of the landscape.

It was not an answer.

There are days when no answer is needed.

[GT]

THE SO-CALLED HEART
TAK ZVANÉ SRDCE
(1963)

TRANSLATED BY IAN MILNER
EWALD OSERS & GEORGE THEINER
WITH ONE POEM TRANSLATED BY
STUART FRIEBERT & DANA HÁBOVÁ

Riders

Over the kind earth twisted like Christmas-bread
over the white earth inscribed grammatically

in nonpareil, brevier, pica,
over the wise earth resounding
like the skull of St Augustine,
over the earth smooth as satin
shrouding the bosom of mystery,

four riders are galloping
on plump white horses,
four rosy-cheeked riders with forget-me-not eyes,
with velvet hands,
with lyres, sugar-basins,
and classics,

one of them lectures,
another one makes love,
the third sings praises,
the fourth gazes into the distance.

The earth undulates slightly behind them,
like the skin of a water snake,
and in the marks of their hooves
grey smallpox erupts.

These will be
the four riders
of the Apocalypse.

[GT]

Discobolus

But
before his final throw
someone whispered to him
from behind
   – Just a moment,
   we still have to discuss this
   purely as a matter of form,
   – You don't know the situation,
   comrade,

   In principle we welcome
   your initiative,
   but you must understand

   – We have to insist on
   fundamental
   agreement
   for every throw,

he felt
the soft Sudanese reed
wind round his wrist,
he wanted to cry out
but
his mouth
was suddenly filled
with the candy-floss of the evening sky,
his muscles swelled
like Thessalian granite,
yet
there was really no point in it,
   – Forward there,
   someone said,
   make way, please,
   Demosthenes
   will throw now,
and Demosthenes
took a grain of sand from under his tongue
and neatly
flicked it in the other's eye,

– Hurrah, one more
world record,
they shouted,

desperate maddened nameless
Discobolus
again swung down
low from the knees,
but he was
already stone
and saw
only a single
huge grain of sand
from horizon to horizon.

So he stood there.

And round the corner
came
the first school excursions
led
by the finest pedagogues,
who referred especially
to the play of the shoulders,
the courageous human heart
and the proud pace forward
on the way
to eternity.

.

[IM]

The new house

No fiery writing on the wall.
No hair
growing out of the ceiling.
No door-knobs
turned by the dead from outside.

No black thoughts in the chimney.
No shadowy chickens in the attic
or under the cupboards.

Far from it.

Latex, vinyl tiles,
elastic dreams,
the kind of house
each of us might
lay a metaphorical brick for.

Only make sure the floors creak,
comrades,
only make sure the floors creak
                        as when the world
                        develops wrinkles,

only make sure the floors creak
when we wander
from room to room,
worried.

[EO]

82

On the building site of a hostel

Among pools of earth,
in a chain reaction of bricks,
between the decaying milk-teeth of concrete blocks

has just been hatched
a grey, two-phase
coffin.

(Wipe your feet)

Enter
a dignified museum
of the gall stones
of emptiness.

(Quiet please)

Fingers of piping explore the hollows
and the Monday morning howl
is everywhere.

(No spitting)

Above the bunk
a single bulb rages
suspended
from a concrete sky.

And on a nail
driven into flesh
shipwrecked socks and brassières
are drying.

(No sliding in the corridors)

We met
staring girls' eyes,
wandering like bugs over the plaster
and we asked,
what is love
and
shall we soon be young?

[GT]

Man cursing the sea

Someone
just climbed to the top of the cliff
and started cursing the sea:

Stupid water, stupid pregnant water,
slimy copy of the sky,
hesitant hoverer between the sun and the moon,
pettifogging reckoner of shells,
fluid, loud-mouthed bull,
fertilising the rocks with his blood,
suicidal sword
splintering itself on any promontory,
hydra, fragmenting the night,
breathing salty clouds of silence,
spreading jelly-like wings
in vain, in vain,
gorgon, devouring its own body,

water, you absurd flat skull of water –

Thus for a while he cursed the sea,
which licked his footprints in the sand
like a wounded dog.

And then he came down
and stroked
the small immense stormy mirror of the sea.

There you are, water, he said,
and went his way.

[GT]

The cat

Outside it was night
like a book without letters.
And the eternal dark
dripped to the stars through the sieve of the city.

I said to her
do not go
you'll only be trapped
and bewitched
and will suffer in vain.

I said to her
do not go
why want
nothing?

But a window was opened
and she went,

a black cat into the black night,
she dissolved,
a black cat in the black night,
she just dissolved

and no one ever saw her again.
Not even she herself.

But you can hear her
sometimes,
when it's quiet
and there's a northerly wind
and you listen intently
to your own self.

[GT]

Fog

The last road has fallen.
From every corner of the breathing fields
the triumphant sea draws nearer
and rocks in its waves
the voices of goldfinches
and the voices of the town.

We are a long way
from space and time,
we come upon the bobbing silhouettes
of stray dinosaurs
and the rayed shadows of Martians
who cannot see for fear.

You have something more to say, but
I do not understand you:
between us stretches
the enormous body of reality
and from its severed head
bubble the clots
of white blood.

[IM]

Night at the observatory

It was thawing.
As if the Avars
were attacking underground.

They stood leaning in the shadows,
his finger discovered
an inch
of unknown gentle country
beneath her left shoulder,

Atlantis, he said,
Atlantis.

Above the fields the wires hissed like iguanas.
A car's horn faded on the air
like a voice from Greek tragedy.
Behind the walls the guard paced back and forth.
Hares were sniffing the distant town.
Wood rotted in the ground.
The Avars were winning.
Trees cracked at the joints.
The wind came and veered off.
They kissed.

From somewhere a rock was falling
its second thousand years.
And the stars were taking in
signals on a frequency of ten megacycles,
beamed to a civilisation
which had died
just before the dawn
of eternity.

[IM]

Prince Hamlet's milk tooth

His tooth fell out milky as
  a dandelion
and everything began to fall,
  as if a rosary had broken,
  as if the string of time had snapped,
and it was downhill going all the way;
round the corner the hearse-driver's coming from his dinner
blind horse in the lead, he jolts along.
Hamlet, we're on our way.

No time now except quickly
  learn to add and multiply,
  learn to cheat and whisper answers,
  to smoke and make love,
  lay in stocks of permanganate
  and naphthalene,
there won't be any more.
And we're on our way, Hamlet.

At dusk you hear the drunken revels of the Danes
  and the trampling of the pollinated flowers,
at dawn the typewriters tap out
  piles of loyalty checks
  with skeleton fingers,
at noon the paper tigers roar
  and commissions are counting up races,
  what will be left for seed
  when it falls.
Hamlet, we're on our way.

But we'll put a bird on our heads
  instead of a soldier's cap, won't we?
We shall walk through the park
  and in the shadow of a red rock
(come in under the shadow of this red rock)
  we shall learn
  to think it over
  just in a small way,
  the way the moss grows,

the way the wash-tubs soak up water,
or we'll take a walk
   five minutes beyond the town,
   growing smaller and smaller,
   a pace-maker on our hearts
   set to an easy rhythm
so we can eat our cake and have it too,
we'll take the oath a little
   and lie a little,
   just from want of not lying,

we heroic lads, salt of the earth,
with our muddled hopes
that one fine day
   we'll damn well prove our salt,
Hamlet.

And keep that tooth of yours.
There won't be any more.

[IM]

Love in August

By an Aztec path
    your hand roamed
    over my chest.
The sun burst out like the egg
    of a pterodactyl
and the aspens rustled
    in a wooden proto-language.
All this has happened before.

The jellied landscape
    was lined with happiness
You worshipped me
    as the goddess of warm rain.

But in every corner of our eyes
    stood one of Maxwell's demons,
allowing the molecules of
    growth and decay
to pass there and back.

And all around us, all around,
    all around,
behind excoriated corneas
    unceasingly,
    like a level behind glass,
    entropy rose
    in a meaningless random universe.

All this has happened before.

All this is yet to happen.

[EO]

And what's new

And what is new in the snow?
Footmarks diverging.
Golden patches, nacre patches,
as on the fleece of butchered lambs.

And what is new in the sand?
Distant cities,
a pillar rising from each.
Some kind of Lot's wife,
turning back,
gently petrifying.

And what is new in the mirror?
Breasts like a pair of calves,
twins of the doe.
And King Solomon
telling lies.

And what is new within?
Like the fine hair-thread of a galvanometer,
like a river's minute source,
someone is thinly laughing.
And therefore exists.

[EO]

What the heart is like

Officially the heart
is oblong, muscular,
and filled with longing.

But anyone who has painted the heart knows
that it is also

spiked like a star
and sometimes bedraggled
like a stray dog at night
and sometimes powerful
like an archangel's drum.

And sometimes cube-shaped
like a draughtsman's dream
and sometimes gaily round
like a ball in a net.

And sometimes like a thin line
and sometimes like an explosion.

And in it is
only a river,
a weir
and at most one little fish
by no means golden.

More like a grey
jealous
loach.

It certainly isn't noticeable
at first sight.

Anyone who has painted the heart knows
that first he had to
discard his spectacles,
his mirror,

throw away his fine-point pencil
and carbon paper

and for a long while
walk
outside.

[EO]

Heart failure

The airport is closed.
The plane circles round like
a fixed idea
over the closed city,
over porters, over dogs,
over troughs, over not-for-sale window-dressing,
over postmen, roosters, and hens,
over brewers and tiny springs.
The airport is closed.

> Tiny Spring, give water
> to my little Rooster:
> He's lying in the yard
> with his feet up –
> I'm scared he'll die.

Water dripping from taps,
the city tumbling down.
There are no matches
for the synthesis of a star.
Somebody has stolen Charon's paddle,
it's strictly forbidden to use the ferry,
the Last Judgment's postponed,
come next week,
spring will be pink
as Aphrodite's arse.
Water dripping from taps.

> Miss Seamstress, give a scarf
> to the tiny Spring, it will
> give water to my little Rooster:
> He's lying in the yard
> with his feet up –
> I'm scared he'll die.

The museum is bulging.
Tiny letters crawl out
like water fleas,
and even the trees scratch themselves.

Drowned dictionaries float.
On top a golden inscription
– Curse Those Who Hate Art –
Down below, the split, tinkered-up
museum is bulging.

Mister Shoemaker, give shoes
to Miss Seamstress,
Seamstress will give a scarf to tiny Spring,
tiny Spring will give water
to my little Rooster:
He's lying in the yard
with his feet up –
I'm scared he'll die.

Tender madness of ashes
in the lungs of the streets.
Black blood of poetry
in the veins of the pavement.
Street cleaners fall behind in their work.
In the madding crowd
somebody knelt down;
So what, they say,
so what, and they're right.
Tender madness of ashes.

Good Swine, give your bristles
to Mister Shoemaker,
Shoemaker will give shoes to Seamstress,
Seamstress will give a scarf to tiny Spring,

tiny Spring will give water
to my little Rooster:
He's lying in the yard
with his feet up –
I'm scared he'll die.

To bear at least one destiny, darling.
You are here but at the same time
you're crying far away.
Home is like a closed
metal rose and dead loves
knock on the roof with little parched fists.

And the one and only tear circles round
as the thirteenth planet,
transparent, uninhabited,
absolutely useless.
To bear at least one destiny.

> Mister Brewer, give the Swine some draff,
> Swine will give her bristle to Shoemaker,
> Shoemaker will give shoes to Seamstress,
> Seamstress will give a scarf to the tiny Spring,
> Spring will give water to –

– Damn it, I can't remember to what...
The empty barrels of heaven rumble
right over our heads,
at night deep down inside
lions roar in thimbles.

and in the cracking of vertebrae
and the yelling of arteries
somebody is singing

> – tiny Spring, give water,
> in the yard, in the yard,
> in the yard, in the yard,

somebody is singing on and on
just like that –

Probably the little rooster.

[SF/DH]

TOTALLY UNSYSTEMATIC ZOOLOGY

ZCELA NESOUSTAVNÁ ZOOLOGIE

(1963)

The end of the world

The bird had come to the very end of its song
and the tree was dissolving under its claws.

And in the sky the clouds were twisting
and darkness flowed through all the cracks
into the sinking vessel of the landscape.

Only in the telegraph wires
a message still
crackled:

C–·–o–––m––e· h···o–––m––e·
y–·–o–––u··– h···a·–v···–e·
a·– s···o–––n–.

[EO]

Death of a sparrow

A sparrow's death
is quite tiny,
grey,
with minute
wiry claws.

And dust
and the end of hopping
is calling now.
And the empty air
is closing its eyes and
calling now.
Mother is picking over
the thinnest good-night squeak and
calling,
a shadow is flying up and
calling,
surely we're not staying here,
roars the setting sun,
quick, soon there'll be decay,
all the world's tenderness
insistently requests,
let's go!

And at that moment
it just isn't
possible.

[EO]

100

Clowns

Where do clowns go?

Where do clowns sleep?

What do clowns eat?

What do clowns do
when no one
but no one at all
laughs any more

Mummy?

[EO]

A boy's head

In it there is a space-ship
and a project
for doing away with piano lessons.

And there is
Noah's ark,
which shall be first.

And there is
an entirely new bird,
an entirely new hare,
an entirely new bumble-bee.

There is a river
that flows upwards.

There is a multiplication table.

There is anti-matter.

And it just cannot be trimmed.

I believe
that only what cannot be trimmed
is a head.

There is much promise
in the circumstance
that so many people have heads.

[IM]

102

WHERE THE BLOOD FLOWS
KAM TEČE KREV
(1963)

Injection

You asked
    what was the meaning of the drop and
    what did the rabbits feel
    when every second
    bore witness against them.

Just look,
    with three-inch boots
    judgement arrives
    and like a voice crying out from the depths
    blood now appears.
    (How else could the heart
    swear an oath?)

And in that glassy silence,
    concurring by a mere movement,
    we feel in our finger-tips
    the weight of life
    and a strange joy in
              being free
                    to ask

Without answers.

[EO]

Suffering

Ugly creatures, ugly grunting creatures,
Completely concealed under the point of the needle,
  behind the curve of the Research Task Graph,
Disgusting creatures with foam at the mouth,
  with bristles on their bottoms,
One after the other
They close their pink mouths
They open their pink mouths
They grow pale
Flutter their legs
  as if they were running a very
  long distance,

They close ugly blue eyes,
They open ugly blue eyes
  and
  they're
  dead.

But I ask no questions,
no one asks any questions.

And after their death we let the ugly creatures
  run in pieces along the white expanse
  of the paper electrophore
We let them graze in the greenish-blue pool
  of the chromatogram
And in pieces we drive them for a dip
  in alcohol
  and xylol
And the immense eye of the ugly animal god
  watches their every move
  through the tube of the microscope
And the bits of animals are satisfied
like flowers in a flower-pot
  like kittens at the bottom of a pond
  like cells before conception.
But I ask no questions,
  no one asks any questions,

Naturally no one asks
Whether these creatures wouldn't have preferred
    to live all in one piece,
    their disgusting life
    in bogs
    and canals,
Whether they wouldn't have preferred to eat
    one another alive,
Whether they wouldn't have preferred to make love
    in between horror and hunger,
Whether they wouldn't have preferred to use
    all their eyes and pores to perceive
    their muddy stinking little world
Incredibly terrified,
Incredibly happy
In the way of matter which can do no more.

But I ask no questions,
    no one asks any questions,
Because it's all quite useless,
Experiments succeed and experiments fail,
Like everything else in this world,
    in which the truth advances
    like some splendid silver bulldozer
    in the tumbling darkness,

Like everything else in this world,
    in which I met a lonely girl
    inside a shop selling bridal veils,
In which I met a general covered
    with oak leaves,
In which I met ambulance men who could find no
    wounded,
In which I met a man who had lost
    his name,
In which I met a glorious and famous, bronze,
    incredibly terrified rat,
In which I met people who wanted to lay down
    their lives and people who wanted to lay down
    their heads in sorrow,
In which, come to think of it, I keep meeting my
    own self at every step.

[GT]

106

Truth

He left, infallible, the door itself
                was bruised as he
                hit the mark.
We two sat awhile
                the figures in the documents
                staring at us like
                green huge-headed beetles
                out of the crevices of evening.
The books stretched
                their spines,
the balance weighed just for the fun of it
                and the glass beads in the necklace
                of the god of sleep whispered together
                in the scales.

'Have you ever been right?' one of us asked.
'I haven't.'

Then we counted on.
It was late
And outside the smokey town, frosty and purple, climbed to the stars.

[GT]

Reality

The small worms of pain still wriggled
    in the limpid air,
The trembling died away and
Something in us bowed low before
    the fact of the operating-table
    the fact of the window
    the fact of space
    the fact of steel
    with seven blades.

The silence was inviolable
    like the surface of a mirror.

Though we wanted to ask
Where the blood was flowing
And
Whether you were still dead,
    darling.

[IM]

ALTHOUGH
AČKOLI
(1969)

Two

Once again
it's the headlong fall
from a crashing astrojet
through the frozen void,
clouds rip the clothes from limbs
and the deafening earth approaches
like a furious new formation,
like the ball from a schizophrenic cannon.

And suddenly – having landed –
and suddenly – broken in two –
and suddenly sunk
one in the other
we are
imprints of earth in earth
and black naphtha gushes from us
river-bed of a chance apartment
and trickles into the eyes
of the avenging angels
pinched in the door-posts.

And then nothing for us
except night
and then nothing for us
except dawn
and the desolate glory of aeronauts
who have lost their wings
in an unknown foreign country.

[IM/JM]

The gift of speech

He spoke:
his round mouth opened
and shut in the manner
of a fish's song.
A bubbling hiss
could be heard
as the void
rushed in headlong
like marsh gas.

[EO]

Oxidation

An invisible flame hovers over the tables.
Eager compounding of elements
of something with nothing,
of something that isn't said
with something that is,
a hidden endothermic filth.

The process continues
in one ear
out of the other,
the brain grinds the poisoned corn
and behind the glass wall a big sewer-rat
swells like
a pink-faced barbers' patron;
gentle, continuous opening of the veins.

We grow, turning to ashes.

And into the wrinkles, monotype
of a body foreign to one's own,
settle the oxides of silence
and the hydroxides of resignation.

Doesn't matter.

There won't be any gold. The philosopher's stone
is not in the plan.
Smoke from the copybooks and drawings falls into the mouth.
Not having words, we applaud.

And inside,
inside this retort of human skin
a huge ashen statue forms,
with tear-rimmed eyes
and white trembling lips
which at night when
roots dance and a star whistles
repeat the empty ashen primeval word
Later Later Later Later.

[IM/JM]

112

The root of the matter

I

Faust
or anyone
clumsy enough to be
       wise,
anyone who bends the nail
       at the first stroke,
anyone who forgets to buy
       his ticket or
       show his pass
       right at the start of the journey,
anyone who can be done out of an ounce
       of his half-pound of butter,
in short Faust
takes a walk
       (before Easter)
beyond the town, stepping into puddles
       he would have rather
       avoided,
strolls against the stream of passers-by, tags on to
       a crowd which
       is cheering, more or less, because
the weather's either cloudy or set fair
       and after all
There is nothing to do
except cheer
       strolls and shares their mood,
            finally
Some mistakes are now mistakes
others are still virtues
       walks around like a grandfather clock
            out of its case and forgetting to chime,
Nothing has happened but we
always saw it coming
       walks around like a run-down battery
            on a movable pavement,
       listens to the voices from above,

Birds of prey do not sing
   listens to the voices from below,
Are you looking for the meaning of life?
And how are you off for garlic?
   he takes the grey road past the cement works,
   he takes the red road past the slaughter-house,
   he takes the blue road past the lake,
   he takes the banned road past the council offices,
   he takes the green road past the playground
            yelling mindless bodies rolling on the ground –
   Youth is no argument.
Age even less
   walks and thinks but rather just
            walks
Thinking is natural
only when there is nothing else
to do

               II

   And at last
            (naturally)
   he meets a black poodle
            running around in smaller and
            smaller circles
like an ominous spider
            spinning its vast web.

   – Look, now we shall see
   the poodle's true kernel,
   the root of the matter,
   says Faust and hurries off
            home.
   And the poodle circles
   like a carrier raven,
For keeping one's balance
wings are best
   like a cat, like a mouse,
   like a black-burning bush,
There is poetry in everything. That
is the biggest argument
against poetry

114

like the ardent hump of the horizon
The hump and other survivals
of the past
and at the same moment the kindly stoniness of the milestone,
Infallibility and other maladies
of adolescence
like the Marathon runner
and yet like himself
(But the root of the matter is not
in the matter itself)
like the demon that denies,
The more negative the type
the more often it says yes
like a fallen angel,
Fall and you shall not
be shaken
like the forefinger of the nether darkness.
But the root of the matter is not
in the matter itself
Faust hurries home,
the circles are growing smaller like the noose
tightening round the neck of a mystery.
And when Faust sees his house before him
he gropes for his always missing
bunch of keys,
ready to make the sign of the cross,
Is the cross more human
than a straight line?
or the sign of the straight line,
From criticism of the straight line we get
the dash
or the sign of the heart,
How many organs are called
heart?
the sign of the heart on the palm,
Heart, yes, but where do we have
the palm?
As he's entering his house
and the poodle's crossing the street eager
as a stone about to become
a star,

suddenly
like a knife that falls
        half-blade into the ground
a bus slips through
and
the poodle's run over and dies.

Faust has the cold shivers,
pushed out of history
by a grain of sand,
by a hundredweight of stupidity.

        III

The root of the matter is not
in the matter itself
        Grandma used to say
        a man who makes no mistakes makes nothing
        but some sort of termite always
                lurks in the kneading-trough
                of every holy eve

Faust lifts the poodle up
and the blood, like a chasuble put on
        over the head,
runs down at his feet

Keys chanced upon he goes and
opens the house and corridor
and study and the evening
confronting the cosmos.

And he sets down the poodle on his opened book
and the letters drink up the blood with gullets unassuaged
        for centuries,
and the pages suck it in through the skin of their unconsciousness
and it is like
a clown's red cap
on the flat skull of literature,
like a set of illuminated
        initials
after the letter Z.

116

IV

Faust, without making light, since pain
      itself gives out the reflected light
      of death,
stands there, nonplussed, and says:
      Dog and nothing but a dog,
      who might have been the allegory of creation
      and are no more than the very meaning of death,
who might have been the annunciator
of another and are no more than
crunched bones,

dog and nothing but a dog, black, white or other,
empty-handed messenger, because there is no
mystery
except the thread which from our hands
leads round the far side of things, round the collar of the landscape
and up the sleeve of a star.
The root of the matter is not
in the matter itself
      dog and nothing but a dog,
      with your eyes gazing into
      the sweet shell of terror,
      stay, you are so fair.
Verweile doch, du bist
so schön
      And Faust feels he loves the dog with a love
      whose essence is hopelessness just as
      hopelessness has its essence in love,
      knows what he should do but cannot,
      not having a bandage
      nor
      a veterinary's licence
      nor
      the right to redress the acts of omnibuses

The root of the matter is not
in the matter itself and often
not
in our hands
    Faust merely knows.
    In the distance a siren wails
        and bells die on the air,
    it is long after Easter,
    Wagner comes in
        to ask after his health,
The good man will live
so that on Judgement Day
he can discourse on the virtues
of naphthalene
    the dog is stretched out and his pupils
        span the horizon
    and the pages of the book beneath him quiver
        like white whispering lips.

And Faust knows
that he will not speak of it,
and if so only by a comma,
only by a word in a big new book.
It is really something like
        a coat of grey fur over the soul,
        like the uniform the unknown soldier
        wears inside him.

And so he goes and starts a painting,
or a gay little song,
or a big new book.
Nothing has happened but we
always saw it coming
    All in all India ink
        is the blood's first sister
    and song is just as final
        as life and death
    and equally without allegory,
        without transcendence
        and without fuss.

[IM]

118

Wisdom

But poetry should never be a thicket,
no matter how delightful, where
the frightened fawn of sense could hide.
        And this is a story of wisdom,
                allied with the roots of life
        And therefore
                in the dark
                and blind.
        A small boy not yet bound
                by the hempen fetters of speech,
        With only ten jingling words
                on his tongue.
        But already in the iron shirt of sickness,
                heavier than a man could bear upright,
        In a white box resembling a glass mountain,
                from which all knights
                tumble head over heel –
There's nothing in the mind that
hasn't been in life.

        (At that time
                tubercular meningitis
                still occurred.)
        On Christmas Eve he got his first
                toys, a giraffe and a red car.
        And in the corridor – far from this
                continent – stood a small Christmas tree
                with tears in its eyes.
There's nothing in life that
hasn't been in the mind.

        And the little boy played, amidst
                symptoms and in the blue valley
                of the fever chart,
        And between two lumbar punctures,
                not unlike to
                being crucified,

He played with his giraffe and his red car,
　　　which represented
　　　his crown jewels of time,
　　　all Christmases and
　　　all the Punches of the world.
And when we asked him
　　　what else he would like
He said with a feverish gaze
　　　from the beyond:
Nothing else.
Wisdom is not in multitude
but in one

　　(At that time
　　　meningitis was still
　　　fatal.)
It was a very white Christmas,
　　　snow down to the roots,
　　　frost up to the sky,
And the glass mountain's tremor
　　　perceptible under our hands.

And he just played.

[EO]

Encyclopaedia: sum of all knowledge

A giant brown-and-white bull
suspended on chains
by his dislocated hind-leg,
its prolapsed belly
contracted in spasm,

is dragged with its twitching mouth along the ground
and slowly butchered
over a leaky sump.

The giant eye, protruded,
is turning inward,

where some fingernail
ceaselessly gropes,
to discover
what is

β-glucuronidase.

[EO]

Annunciation

It could have been a stray neighing of the night
        outside beneath the window
        as the fire burnt low.
It could have been Jericho's trumpets,
it could have been a chorus
        of hunchbacks under the snow,
it could have been an oak's word to the willows,
and it could have been the pecking of a mocking-bird
        under an owl's wing.
It could have been the judgement of an archangel
and it could have been a newt's evil prophecy.
It could have been the weeping of our only love.

But the functionary at the table turned to us
        and said:
Listen: It is necessary for you to listen.
Listen more resolutely.
let us listen, listen, he listens,
they listen, more resolutely,
more resolutely listen,
lis ten lis ten,
LISTEN,
L i s t e n to us –

And so we didn't hear a damn thing.

[IM/JM]

We who laughed

We were expelled
from the classroom, the square,
gaming-house,
stock exchange, market-place,
television screen and
gilt frame,
and from any
history,
    we
        who laughed.

The city swelled in importance
by two floors
and the phone-tapping devices
tapped better
(in the silence)
and the gatekeeper
kept better guard
and love reached for a knife
and the knife reached for blood
(in the silence)
and the rats became still more
like rats (who never laugh)
while we were expelled,
    we
        who laughed.
Some pterodactyls
circled the heavy sky
and horsetail and club-moss
grew in the flower-pots
and an elegiac mastodon
watched from the town hall
to see if we were returning
    we
        who laughed.

We were not returning.
We walked the worn paving-stones
of the unending street

between the warehouse and the factories,
between the machine-tool shop and the scrap heaps,
between the graffiti walls
and the empty houses,
steps, steps, steps,
through the spindled space
between bushes, between molehills
and
minefields
and
someone stumbled
in the silence . . . and then nothing. Only silence.
That's why we laughed.

[IM/JM]

Lyric mood

The little elephant Pete ambles in porcelain.
The spacious swallow is circling the conduit.

We follow the flight of the Tunguz meteorite through a rose
and the termite's path to the stars.

We went through a whole gay library of puppets
and a whole sad library of puppets.

We examined a cake raisin by raisin
and schoolgirls' eyes pupil by pupil.

For a long time I walked alone:
tree, root, root, root-fibres, clay,
stone, clay, clay, clay, bone,
banned road,
call to lunch.

Phantoms, illusion, illusion, smoke and fumes,
lightning, nothing, nothing, announcing
the official load-line for tomorrow.

Lettering on the bookshelf,
mouse in the art gallery.

In the heavens: any bastard looks like
Davy Crockett.
In the depths: a demon in every pancake.

I haven't found anything,
but I can say so.

Although...

[IM/JM]

Anatomy of a leap into the void

A.   Use of the lift
     going up
     is permitted, provided

B.   Use of the lift
     going down
     is not permitted, provided

C.   Use of the lift
     going up is

D.   Use of the lift
     going down is not

E.   Use of the lift
     going up

F.   Use of the lift
     going

G.   Use of the lift

H.   Is   Is not

I.   Use

J.   U--

[EO]

126

The Prague of Jan Palach

And here stomp Picasso's bulls.
And here march Dali's elephants on spidery legs.
And here beat Schönberg's drums.
And here rides Señor de la Mancha.
And here the Karamazovs are carrying Hamlet.
And here is the nucleus of the atom.
And here is the cosmodrome of the Moon.
And here stands a statue without the torch.
And here runs a torch without the statue.
And it's all so simple. Where
Man ends, the flame begins –
And in the ensuing silence can be heard the crumbling
of ash worms. For
those milliards of people, taken by and large,
are keeping their traps shut.

[GT]

Without title

Certainly we can read in the nettles and
     savour Marcel Proust.
Certainly we can make antibodies
     to three-time, as we play eeny meeny miny mo.
Certainly we can pay reparations to the Scythians.

Certainly we can consider the north star
     a special case of a slipped stitch.
Certainly we can carry grandpa in a cone to market
     with vanilla and superphosphate.
Certainly we can exchange John of Luxemburg
     for a couple of tip-cat sticks.
Certainly we can swallow all the cockchafers tell us
     about the sexual life of skulls.

Certainly we can bark and copulate under the new
     moon.
Certainly we can ferment milk in Patagonia.
Certainly we can swear we aren't alive,
     that we shan't be alive and never were.

Certainly we can trickle out of the smallest hole
     in a horse chestnut.

If only someone, as far as possible the good Lord
     or His responsible Deputy,
      would tell us the meaning of
Certainly
     and the meaning of
Can.

[IM/JM]

128

Although

Although a poem arises when there's nothing else to be done, although a poem is a last attempt at order when one can't stand disorder any longer,

although poets are most needed when freedom, vitamin C, communications, laws and hypertension therapy are also most needed,

although to be an artist is to fail and art is fidelity to failure, as Samuel Beckett says,

a poem is not one of the last but one of the first things of man.

*

Although a poem is only a little word machine/ as William Carlos Williams says/ a little word machine ticking in the world of megamachines and megatons and megaelectronvolts,

although in the world of a poem one doesn't live any better than in any other world, although the world of a poem is dreary, arises out of desolation and perishes in the desolation of spiritual history,

although art doesn't solve problems but rather only wears them out, as Susan Sontag says,

yet a poem is the only sword and shield:

for in principle and essence it is not against tyrants, against automobiles, against madness and cancer and the gates of death, but against what is there all the time, all the time inside and out, all the time in front, behind, and in the middle, all the time with us and against us.

It is against emptiness. A poem is being as against emptiness. Against the primary and secondary emptiness.

*

The limits of emptiness: emptiness begins where the limits of man end. The limits of man as the principle of arranging and determining, seeing and conceiving a plan against the entropy of dead things. The limits of man expand and contract, pulse with his energy.

And emptiness is greatest where man was rather than where he was not. Interstellar space is not empty, but there is no worse emptiness than a house in ruins.

Or a thought that has come to nothing.

Observing the stars, we experience an emptiness which is not theirs.

*

Emptiness doesn't approach like a catastrophe or torrent. Emptiness seeps. Seeps through an unrepaired roof or a filthy desk. Emptiness seeps through cracks in roads and cracks in dreams. The master-key which opens emptiness is called I couldn't care less.

Emptiness is not knowledge of impotence but the demand for impotence. Admission of the claim to impotence. The will to impotence.

Emptiness is the drops we ourselves consider to be the flood which according to law is to come after us.

*

And emptiness is not the concern of the single person, of the isolated individual. By its aspect of disorderliness it becomes the affair of all, concretises itself as life environment, is inhaled, infects, multiplies, epidemicises.

Its focus is where there are no self-purifying forces of any stable inter-human order, where there is no relying either on history or ancient beauty or a new powerful image of life. Where things and thoughts depend entirely on new creation and a newly imprinted order and where there is no perfection in the new creation nor stability in the order.

*

I certainly don't think that our being is essence, the thing is to fill our being with essence; in that 'is to', in that 'is necessary', we actually are. Or I am.

But what a peculiar relationship exists between what is and what ought to be, between being and the fulfilment of being. A dream is what transcends existence and the dreamer. A dream is what ought to be. But with the first step towards a dream's fulfilment, its realisation and therefore transcendence, its content is no longer the mere expression of human freedom but a symptom of obligation. And obligations go very hard with us, though they are the fruits of our freedom: how exceptional it is to finish a book with the same feeling of perfection as that with which it was begun. How difficult it is to continue a friendship with the same purity as at the beginning. How difficult it is to finish building a shed with boards of the same size as the first two.

There is tension not only between reality and dream, but between dream and the realisation of dream.

And in stretched seams, emptiness arises.

Tension, which leads to fulfilment, continues above what is realised.

Tension lasts and petrifies. Hardens. Becomes a stable sign and organ. It is no longer mere stimulus but also resignation.

And in hardened seams, emptiness arises.

We demand freedom also in regard to what we have freely chosen. But this freedom goes against itself. This freedom means confinement in the approximate, the impossible, the unreal; confinement in futility.

And is this what is human? Where does this feeling, and in the end conception, of the human come from? Of the human which exists in a self-contradicting freedom, in the freedom to betray our dreams and the beginnings of self-realisation, in the freedom to betray our order. In the freedom that goes against one of the few evidences of self-realisation, against the evidence of science in the broadest sense of the word.

This romantic human is not human, but a retreat from the human. It is not a fulfilment of being, but a regression to being without needs, without fulfilment, without essence.

*

Freedom is not the return to emptiness but fullness of being. Freedom is not regression from integration and determinacy but realisation of the higher forms of relatedness. And dependence. In the reverse case a new-born child would be more free than Beethoven or Comenius; and an opossum than a new-born child.

Freedom is the goal and therefore also the bond of culture and civilisation; the freedom that is sought in regression to the past conditions of mankind and men is a *contradictio in adiecto*: otherwise why did we take on all the wear and tear of humanising apes?

Freedom, as the search for higher forms of determining the human, certainly presupposes the fully developed consciousness of modern man, not the intoxicated sub-cortex of the human brain nor any unrestrained individuality foot-loose in the primal nature of lightning, putrefaction and termites, wild flowers and mating. Similarly we cannot manipulate the collective mind of citizens so that it fiddles with itself as it would with a TV set. Or with politics.

Freedom – so easily defined as the negative measure of tyranny – is the new definition of man in society and of man and society, freedom is self-regulation, self-regulation more difficult and more exacting than the intrigues of a tyrant. The demand for freedom, which turns against tyrants and parkways, against physical jerks and political economy, turns also against itself and nothing else; and so makes things very easy for tyrants.

A marathon runner is more free than a vagabond, and a cosmonaut than a sage in the state of levitation. Otherwise it would be more consistent to bark than write poems and to live in a leprosery than in San Francisco. Or Prague.

*

Certainly a poem is only a game.

Certainly a poem exists only at the moment of origin and at the moment of reading. And at best in the shadow-play of memory.

Certainly one can't enter the same poem twice.

Certainly a poet has the impression from the beginning that no purpose exists, as Henry Miller has said.

Certainly art becomes generally acceptable only when it declines into a mechanism and its order becomes a habit.

But in its aimlessness, in its desperate commitment to the word, in its primal order of birth and re-birth, a poem remains the most general guarantee that we can still do something, that we can still do something against emptiness, that we haven't given in but are giving ourselves *to* something.

The most general guarantee that we are not composed only of facts, of facts which, as Ernst Fischer says, are deeds withered into things.

Provided a poem, which is the poet's modest attempt to put off disintegration for a while, is not regarded as the philosopher's stone, bringing salvation and deliverance to stupefied mankind.

For art doesn't solve problems but only wears them out.

For art is fidelity to failure.

For a poem is when nothing else remains.

Although...

[IM/JM]

132

CONCRETE
BETON
(1970)

Subway station

This evening   Mr Howard T. Lewis,
of unknown address,   gloomy and tired,
wearing a grey overcoat and brown hat,
having decided to take   the BMT, Canarsie Line,
met   at the last station on 8th Ave.
a man   in a grey overcoat and brown hat
whose face,   gloomy and tired, was
the face of Mr   Howard T. Lewis,
while by the barrier   at the end of the empty platform
stood a man   in a grey overcoat, of gloomy appearance,
whose face   was also the face
of Howard T. Lewis   and   gazed dumbly
at the bottom of the dirty steps   down which came
a man in a brown hat,   gloomy and tired,
with a face that was the face of Howard T. Lewis.

And then   through the worn wooden spokes
of the turnstile   came a woman, tired and gloomy,
of unknown address   with a handbag and in a brown
hat   whose face was the face
of all men   and therefore also of Howard T. Lewis and
the steps in the distance   and the nervously muffled steps
near by, steps   of figures bowed by the murkiness
and pale from the light were the steps
of Howard T. Lewis, steps   from an unknown address
to   an unknown address,   now and then
the turnstile turned again   with a snap like a head
dropping in the basket,   or behind the barrier
could be seen   a figure without sex and of no
address,   but otherwise completely like
Howard T. Lewis,   steps   were heard,
heads,   spokes,   distances,   lights   and tunnels
sucked in the sign   8th Ave.   8th Ave.   8th Ave.
in droning crescendo.

When the train left   a stray wind
scattered the pages of a paper   in which there was a report on
      the unknown
address,   fate   and identification
of a man   in a grey overcoat and brown hat,
gloomy and tired.

[IM/JM]

Bull fight

Someone runs about,
someone scents the wind,
someone stomps the ground, but it's hard.

Red flags flutter
and on his old upholstered jade the picador
with infirm lance
scores the first wound.

Red blood spurts between the shoulder-blades.

Chest about to split,
tongue stuck out to the roots.
Hooves stomp of their own accord.

Three pairs of the bandoleros in the back.
And a matador is drawing his sword
over the railing.

And then someone (blood-spattered, all in)
stops and shouts:
Let's go, quit it,
let's go, quit it,
let's go over across the river and into the trees,
let's go across the river and into the trees,
let's leave the red rags behind,
let's go some other place,

thus he shouts,
or wheezes,
or whispers,

and the barriers roar and
no one understands because
everyone feels the same about it,

the black-and-red bull is going to fall
and be dragged away,
and be dragged away,
and be dragged away,

without grasping the way of the world,
without having grasped the way of the world,
before he has grasped the way of the world.

[IM/JM]

Planet

The module made more like a crash-landing.
And on the planet – only fused rocks
and tinder, no spark of life.

Booming.

But the first guards were murdered.
The bodies gored by fangs
were buried in vain. In the black daylight
they vanished immediately from the stone graves
and next day attacked the living.

They felt that some sort of principle,
vampire in spirit, was waiting here to use
the bodies, brains and thoughts
for ends which, like darkness, like spin, like laughter,
were fathomless.

And others were devoured and others
among the gored dead stalked the living.
Until it was no longer clear who
still had the original life in him.

The planet stood like the howling of wolves
petrified in timelessness.

There was no point in pretending to be crabs.
They knew, and it knew through them.
They repaired the module and set out for Earth.
Perhaps still human, perhaps also vampires.

And it's not known whether they ever landed.
And it's not known what did land here.
Maybe there are only
symptoms. And booming.
And the strange activity of dead idiots.

[IM/JM]

The jesters

They jumped. They stamped the ground.
Shrank. Crawled through the retina.
Swelled. Got stuck
        in an indicative clause.

They growled. They sang.
Founded a flea circus
and crawled into it.

They blossomed. They wilted.
Flew in a pumpkin and down a hair.
So that
        they reached the roots.

They rang the bell. They put the lights out.
Dodged the curtain calls.
Gobbled up cap and bells.
Consequently
        they were appointed

supervisors of the Clowns.

[IM/JM]

AFTER

ON THE CONTRARY
NAOPAK
(1982)

TRANSLATED BY EWALD OSERS

Brief reflection on cats growing in trees

When moles still had their annual general meetings
    and when they still had better eyesight it befell
    that they expressed a wish to discover what
    was above.
So they elected a commission to ascertain what was above.
The commission despatched a sharp-sighted fleet-footed
    mole. He, having left his native mother earth,
    caught sight of a tree with a bird on it.

Thus a theory was put forward that up above
    birds grew on trees. However,
    some moles thought this was
    too simple. So they despatched another
    mole to ascertain if birds did grow on trees.

By then it was evening and on the tree
    some cats were mewing. Mewing cats,
    the second mole announced, grew on the tree.
Thus an alternative theory emerged about cats.

The two conflicting theories bothered an elderly
    neurotic member of the commission. And he
    climbed up to see for himself.
By then it was night and all was pitch-black.

Both schools are mistaken, the venerable mole declared.
    Birds and cats are optical illusions produced
    by the refraction of light. In fact, things above

Were the same as below, only the clay was less dense and
    the upper roots of the trees were whispering something,
    but only a little.

And that was that.

Ever since the moles have remained below ground:
    they do not set up commissions
    or presuppose the existence of cats.

Or if so only a little.

Brief reflection on accuracy

Fish
  always accurately know where to move and when,
  and likewise
  birds have an accurate built-in time sense
  and orientation.

Humanity, however,
  lacking such instincts resorts to scientific
  research. Its nature is illustrated by the following
  occurrence.

A certain soldier
  had to fire a cannon at six o'clock sharp every evening.
  Being a soldier he did so. When his accuracy was
  investigated he explained:

I go by
  the absolutely accurate chronometer in the window
  of the clockmaker down in the city. Every day at seventeen
  forty-five I set my watch by it and
  climb the hill where my cannon stands ready.
  At seventeen fifty-nine precisely I step up to the cannon
  and at eighteen hours sharp I fire.

And it was clear
  that this method of firing was absolutely accurate.
  All that was left was to check that chronometer. So
  the clockmaker down in the city was questioned about
  his instrument's accuracy.

Oh, said the clockmaker,
  this is one of the most accurate instruments ever. Just imagine,
  for many years now a cannon has been fired at six o'clock sharp.
  And every day I look at this chronometer
  and always it shows exactly six.

So much for accuracy.
  And fish move in the water, and from the skies
  comes a rushing of wings while

Chronometers tick and cannon boom.

Brief reflection on the theory of relativity

Albert Einstein, in conversation –
  (Knowledge is discovering
  what to say) – in conversation one day
  with Paul Valéry,
  was asked:

Mr Einstein, how do you work
  with your ideas? Do you note them down
  the moment they strike you? Or only
  at night? Or the morning?

Albert Einstein replied:
  Monsieur Valéry, in our business
  ideas are so rare that
  if a man hits upon one
  he certainly won't forget it.

Not in a year.

Brief reflection on the word Pain

Wittgenstein says: the words 'It hurts' have replaced
    tears and cries of pain. The word 'Pain'
    does not describe the expression of pain but replaces it.
    Thus it creates a new behaviour pattern
    in the case of pain.

The word enters between us and the pain
    like a pretence of silence.
    It is a silencing. It is a needle
    unpicking the stitch
    between blood and clay.

The word is the first small step
    to freedom
    from oneself.

In case others
    are present.

Brief reflection on an old woman with a barrow

Given an old woman and given a barrow.
I.e. the system old woman O and barrow B.

The system is moving from the paved yard Y to the corner C,
    from the Corner C to the stone S, from the stone S
    to the forest F, from the forest F to the horizon H.

The horizon H is the point where vision ends
    and memory begins.

Nevertheless the system is moving
    at a constant velocity v,
    along a constant path,
    through a constant world and
    a constant destiny,
renewing its impulse and its meaning
    from within itself.

A relatively independent system:
in landscapes from horizon to horizon
always just one old woman with a barrow.

And thus we have, once and for all,
    that geodetic unit, the
    unit of travel there and back, the
    unit of autumn, the
    unit Our daily bread, the
    unit of wind and lowering sky, the
    unit of the distance home, the
    unit As we forgive them, the
    unit of nightfall, the
    unit of footsteps and dust, the
    unit of life-fulfilment Amen.

Brief reflection on Johnny

The above-named, as is well-known, coming
    from a poor but honest background,
    set out across nine mountains and nine
    rivers to see the world.

There
    he became a victim of myths. In reality,
    as of course we all know, he did
    in the Black Forest meet the white old man and exchange
    a few words with him;

However,
    he gave him nothing since by then his cake had been
    polished off by the dwarfs.
    He went on, sadly, into the city but
    he couldn't hear any story in any tavern
    since

All taverns had been closed by royal decree
    and strangers, after questioning under duress,
    were speedily escorted to the Dragon's Rock.

There he met the dragon which, without further ado,
    gave him a thrashing and made him sign a contract
    that he would lure all passing knights-at-arms
    into the dragon's claws.

The princess and half the kingdom were things he had to
    invent when he was captured on his flight
    by musketeers and when he had to explain
    his lengthy absence.

And so he came back home impoverished and emaciated,
    in rags and totally without illusions. He sat down
    amidst the hay in contemplation. It was then
    that he discovered all of a sudden
    he understood the speech of birds and flies,

And listened to them with complete comprehension.

And from the red-backed shrikes he learned
    some really pretty fairy-tales.

Brief reflection on Charlemagne

(see Julius Zeyer's tale of the same)

Outside the gate
hangs a bell. Charlemagne, son of Pepin the Short,
had it placed there. Those who have suffered injustice
strike it and Charles interrupts his king-business,
receives them at once, hears them out, and dispenses justice.
That was in AD 800.

This year the bell rang.
In the rain, which was
a cloudburst rather than a drizzle
and had been continuing for eleven hundred years,
soaked to the skin, drenched, like a drowned rat,
in a fool's motley
stood Charlemagne.

In broken Frankish he urgently pleaded
for a hearing.

Brief reflection on cracks

Something cracks every moment because
    everything cracks one day, an egg,
    armour, a book's spine.

The human spine may be
    the only exception, though
    much depends on pressure, time and place.
    Such cases are therefore rare.
    Hardly any. Because
    there are so many pressures, places and times
    around.

Cracks are normally stuck together. It is not on record
    that anyone would want to go about cracked,
    not even the whip-crackers.

Cracks are mended with wax, paraffin,
    soldered, bandaged. Or talked out of existence. This most of all.

But a mended egg is no longer an egg,
    soldered armour is no longer armour,
    a bandaged heel is an Achilles' heel and
    a man talked out of existence is not the man he was,
    rather the Achilles' heel of others.

Worst of all is when hundreds of mended eggs
    pass themselves off as best eggs and hundreds
    of suits of soldered armour as true armour,
    thousands of cracked people as monoliths.

Then it's all one huge crack.

All we can do in the world of cracks is
    now and then to call out, Mr Director, mind your step on the stairs,
    you have a crack, sir, if I may say so.

That's all. Afterwards there's only more cracking.

[IM/JM]

Brief reflection on gargoyles

In the course of general petrifaction cliffs grow
    from diatoms, cities from sighs and
    imperatives from question-marks.

In the course of general petrifaction angels resident
    in pointed-arch portals, among finials and
    slender turrets rigidify into solid
    sulphurous devils, with desperate claws catch hold of
    cornices and thus become gargoyles.

In this role
    they start to open their mouths at those passing
    below, saying:

What are you gaping at, clot,
    or else
Dust thou art, to dust returnest,
    or sometimes
Better watch your gravitation.

When it rains they pour out their spite in copious streams,
    shaking with pleasure and contempt,
at night they lick the earth with spongy tongues,
    turning white into black
    and vice versa.

But sometimes in spring they feel ashamed of themselves,
    climb down, and in the shape of black cats and
    moon-struck dormice
    with yowls they criticise the Gothic style and
    gargoyles in particular. Then inquisitive angels
    without portfolios descend from on high
    and, clinging to the cornices with desperate claws,
    they listen. And so they, too, go rigid
    and sulphurous, and petrify.

The above procedure thus ensures
a perpetual exchange of gargoyles,
the unchangeability of Gothic façades
and a respect among all passers-by, cats and dormice

for gravitation.

Brief reflection on killing the Christmas carp

You take a kitchen-mallet
and a knife
and hit
the right spot, so it doesn't jerk, for
jerking means only complications and reduces profit.

And the watchers already narrow their eyes, already admire the
          dexterity,
already reach for their purses. And paper is ready
for wrapping it up. And smoke rises from chimneys.
And Christmas peers from windows, creeps along the ground
and splashes in barrels.

Such is the law of happiness.

I am just wondering if the carp is the right creature.

A far better creature surely would be one
which – stretched out – held flat – pinned down –
would turn its blue eye
on the mallet, the knife, the purse, the paper,
the watchers and the chimneys
and Christmas,

And quickly

say something. For instance

These are my happiest days; these are my golden days.
Or
The starry sky above me and the moral law within me,
Or
And yet it moves.

Or at least
Hallelujah!

Brief reflection on laughter

In laughter we stretch the mouth from ear to ear,
    or at least in that direction,
    we bare our teeth and in that way reveal
    long-past stages in evolution
    when laughter still was an expression of
    triumph over a slain neighbour.

We expel our breath right up from the throat,
    according to need we gently vibrate our
    vocal chords, if necessary we also touch our foreheads
    or the back of our heads, or we rub our hands or slap
    our thighs, and in that way reveal long-past stages
    when victory also presupposed
    fleetness of foot.

Generally speaking, we laugh when we feel like laughing.

In special instances we laugh
    when we don't feel like laughing at all,
    we laugh because laughter is prescribed or
    we laugh because it isn't prescribed.

And so, in effect, we laugh all the time, if only
to conceal the fact that all the time someone
is laughing at us.

Brief reflection on the Flood

We have been brought up with the notion that
  a flood means
  water rising beyond all bounds,
  engulfing fields and woodlands, hills and mountains,
  places of temporary and abiding stay,
so that
  men and women, meritorious oldsters
  and babes in arms, as well as the creatures of field and forest,
  creepies and heebee-jeebies,
  huddle together on rocky pinnacles
  which slowly sink into the steel-grey waves.

And only some Ark...and only
  some Ararat...Who knows.
  Reports on the causes of floods differ most
  strangely. History itself is a science
  that's based on poor memory.

That kind of flood needn't worry us too much.

A real flood
  looks more like a puddle.
  Like a little swamp nearby.
  Like a leaky washtub.
  Like silence.
  Like nothing.

A real flood means that balloon-bubbles
  come from our mouths
  and we think they are
  words.

Brief reflection on test-tubes

Take
    a piece of fire, a piece of water,
    a piece of a rabbit or a piece of a tree,
    or any piece of a human being,
    mix it, shake it, stopper it up,
    keep it warm, in the dark, in the light, refrigerated,
    let it stand still for a while – yourselves far from still –
    but that's the real joke.

After a while
    you look – and it's growing,
    a little ocean, a little volcano,
    a little tree, a little heart, a little brain,
    so little you don't hear it lamenting
    as it wants to get out,
    but that's the real joke, not hearing it.

Then go
    and record it, all dashes or
    all crosses, some with exclamation-marks,
    all noughts and all figures, some with exclamation-marks,
    and that's the real joke, in effect a test-tube
    is a device for changing noughts
    into exclamation-marks.

That's the real joke
    which makes you forget for a while
    that really you yourself are

In the test-tube.

Brief reflection on light

We make light so we can see.

In the Silurian they made light to see the Silurian.
In the Diluvium they made light to see the Diluvium.
In Troy they made light to see Troy.
And that's how they spotted all those Greeks around them.
In the Enlightenment they made light to see the Enlightenment.

The same applies today.

Indeed
certain species developed, such as fireflies,
or occupations, such as torch-bearers.
A lot of energy is converted into light,
electrical and chemical, mechanical and biological.
Even a battery is sometimes found.
So much light has developed that we can see round corners,
that we can see into our stomachs,
that we can see into the little roots of night.

Not that seeing is any particular
fun.
But we've got to see in order to
make light,
       light,
              light,
until we go blind.

The Minotaur's thoughts on poetry

Certainly this thing exists. For
on dark nights when, unseen,
I walk through the snail-like windings of the street
the sound of my own roar reaches me
from a great distance.

Yes. This thing exists. For surely
even cicadas were once of gigantic stature
and today you can find mammoths' nests
under a pebble. The earth, of course,
is lighter than it once was.

Besides, evolution is nothing but
a long string of false steps;
and it may happen that a severed head
will sing.

And it's not due, as many believe, to
the invention of words. Blood
in the corners of the mouth is substantially
more ancient and the cores of the rocky planets
are heated by the grinding of teeth.

Certainly this thing exists.
Because
a thousand bulls want to be
human.
And vice versa.

Brief reflection on maps

Albert Szent-Gyorgi, who knew a thing or two about maps,
   by which life moves somewhere or other,
   used to tell this story from the war,
   through which history moves somewhere or other:

From a small Hungarian unit in the Alps a young lieutenant
   sent out a scouting party into the icy wastes.
   At once
   it began to snow, it snowed for two days and the party
   did not return. The lieutenant was in distress: he had sent
   his men to their deaths.

On the third day, however, the scouting party was back.
   Where had they been? How had they managed to find their way?
   Yes, the men explained, we certainly thought we were
   lost and awaited our end. When suddenly one of our lot
   found a map in his pocket. We felt reassured.
   We made a bivouac, waited for the snow to stop, and then
      with the map
   found the right direction.
   And here we are.

The lieutenant asked to see that remarkable map in order to
   study it. It wasn't a map of the Alps
   but the Pyrenees.

Goodbye.

Brief reflection on death

Many people act
as if they hadn't been born yet. Meanwhile, however,
William Burroughs, asked by a student
if he believed in life after death,
replied:
– And how do you know you haven't died yet?

Brief reflection on childhood

In the turquoise-coloured fields of childhood there's nothing
   except childhood.

Nor is there anything in the yellowing sky, nor
   on the bare ochre wall, nor behind the bare ochre wall,
   nor on the oriental horizon, nor beyond the horizon,
   nor in the little house, nor on the target, nor in the mirror,
   nor behind the mirror.

Except childhood.

Objects are strange and unfamiliar because they were there
   before and will be there after. So far as I remember,
   childhood is solitude amidst
   a confederacy of things and creatures which
   have no name or purpose.

Names and purpose are thought up by us afterwards. Then we believe
   that the wall divides something from something else,
   that the house provides shelter from stormy weather and
   that the nightingale spreads happiness by song and fairy-tales.

That's what we believe. But it probably isn't so.

For the emptiness of houses is boundless, boundless
   the fierceness of nightingales, and the path from gate
   to gate has no end anywhere.

And seeking we lose, discovering we conceal.
For we are still searching for our childhood.

Brief reflection on fence

A fence
   begins nowhere
   ends nowhere
and
   separates the place where it is
   from the place where it isn't.

Unfortunately, however,
   every fence is relatively
   permeable, some for small
   others for large things, so that
the fence actually
   does not separate but indicates
   that something should be separated.
   And that trespassers will be prosecuted.

In this sense
   the fence can
   perfectly well be replaced
   with an angry word, or sometimes even
   a kind word, but that as a rule
   does not occur to anyone.

In this sense therefore
   a truly perfect fence
   is one
   that separates nothing from nothing,
   a place where there is nothing,
   from a place where there's also nothing.

That is the absolute fence, similar to the poet's word.

Brief reflection on eyes

Goddesses, gods, fear and Twiggy have very large eyes.
Some gods, in fact, have such large eyes that nothing was left for
    anything else and that god *is* the eye.
The Eye itself then sees everything, knows everything, and grants
        gifts
which admittedly would be granted even without the Eye, but with
    the Eye they're a lot better.

Cyclopses, olms, informers and the angels of the Apocalypse have
very small eyes. But a lot of them.
One small eye at every keyhole.
Certain angels and their equals in rank, by which we don't mean
        the olms,
have such small eyes that not even a fragment of man
fits into them.
These eyes then drop their lids for concealment.

Behind the eyes are the optic tracts and the occipital lobes of the
        brain,
where individual areas correspond to individual areas of the retina.

Behind excessively large eyes lies nothing.
Behind excessively small eyes sits the Apocalypse.

Brief reflection on the sun

Thanks to the systematic work of our meteorologists,
and altogether thanks to the general labour effort,
we have all been witnesses of many solstices,
    solar eclipses and even
    sunrises.

But we have never seen the sun.

It's like this: we have seen the sun
    through the trees, the sun above the Tatra
    National Park, the sun beyond a rough road,
    the sun drenching Hašek's village of Lipnice,
but not the sun,
Just-the-Sun.

Just-the-Sun, of course, is unbearable.
Only the sun related to trees, shadows,
    hills, Lipnice and the Highway Department
is a sun for people.

The Just-the-Sun hangs like a fist over the ocean,
    over the desert or over the airliner,
    it doesn't cast shadows, it doesn't flicker from movement,
    and is so unique it almost isn't at all.

And it's just the same with truth.

Brief reflection on dwarfs

In the far world
a great many dwarfs
have become by far the greatest
dwarfs in the world.

Already a Superlohengrin approaches
on a superswan, to the choir of a
supercigar which has acquired
the permanent wedding march.
Geological strata of petrified
dreams and words thunder underfoot.

In the near world
a barely perceptible
Snow White drags herself along mouse tracks,
searching for seven honest old
dwarfs,

such as would
still feel ashamed
under the magnifying glass.

The dangers of the night

Bedroom; a double bed; ceiling; bedside table; radio.
And outside darkness propped up by the trees
beneath which a dark blue jaguar is prowling.

The walls part and the double helix
of oneness
pervades the shadowy breathing of the roof.

Perhaps a galaxy. But more probably
the whites of eyes giving a hint of wind.

The enemy is approaching: the black image,
the image of oneself
in the mirror, sleep. His hands
are growing and his fingertips are
touching.

Resist. For in the morning,
in the naive light of songbirds' brains,
he that wakes will be
someone else.

Attempted assassination

He walks through the town like
an indigestible remnant
on the tongue. Ticking away in his pocket
is the infernal machine, to be
flung or placed
at the right moment, at the right spot.

His shadow appears to him
like a fuse-cord stretching
through history, from war to war.
His body appears to him
like the fulcrum of a balance
on which our age
tips the scales

and centuries shall be put
to flight.

He clutches his infernal machine
to his heart, closer and closer,
so it dissolves his skin,
so it dissolves its metal,
the one permeating the other.

Now the infernal machine is inside,
and ticking and ticking, and when
it at last seems that this is the street,
and this is the house, and this is the moment
in the funeral cortège of our days
he reaches inside, but
it can no longer be pulled out,
yet it is ticking, and hurting,
and he takes to his heels,
fleeing from the ticking,
fleeing from himself,
losing his shadow and losing the town,

finding himself on the plateau
of an unsetting sun,
an unmoving sky, and
immersing himself in the settling
precipitate of clay,
leaving an outline

of body or explosion,
a temporary body and a permanent explosion.

On Sunday a family
takes a walk in those parts.
Can you hear it? asks the little boy,
poking a stick in the clay.

No one hears anything.

Drop it this instant,
says the father to the boy
who in his hand triumphantly
carries

a dead mouse.

Theatre

Only sorcerers believe that the theatre is a mingling of the blood of the poet with the blood of the actor. The simple magic of the theatre is in the fact that an empty space which signifies nothing is entered by people with tickets and by people who tear off the tickets, and by people in overcoats and people without overcoats, and by people who know it all by heart and by people who don't know it by heart yet.

They have all read the inscription THEATRE and for a while they act accordingly.

For that period of time everything signifies something. Even the space, even the hush, even the breath, even the blood, even the shadow.

One of the troubles with the world is that the inscription THEATRE is found in so few places.

The Minotaur's loneliness

Walls. Walls. A voice. A word
uttered weeks before returns
years later,
with its other self.

Walls. Walls. Fear. Shadow
of a shadow fearing a shadow.
As we...Do not forgive.

Walls. Walls. Fragments of fragments,
amphorae from which for seven years trickled
images of seas dried up but for their roar.

Walls. Walls. And perhaps
not even walls. Perhaps I'm merely walking
on an imaginary ground-plan,
unable to do otherwise:

To turn aside would mean there was no Minos,
there was no Crete, there was no Theseus.
Only an ageing Ariadne
on the cliff's edge awaiting
her fall.

Minotaurus Faber

Whenever I come to the table
I neatly lay out my tools
(small hammers, pliers, anvils and small shafts),
I draw a diagram, in red and black,
upon the infinite white surface of beginning,
I start to join and bend, rivet and solder,
hammer and scrape, the blows ring out
from depth of soul to depth of soul,
concentric rings are widening and I
am at the centre, at the very centre.

Already a small machine is taking shape,
a fledgling machine, transmissions, firing-pins,
windings and spools, attraction and repulsion,
here and there it ticks, here and there
it listens,
we're nearly there,

when from down under me rings out the sound of hooves
pounding upon the savage granite
like drums in black festivities,
hammering of arteries, tightening of muscle and the pull
of tendon straps (hands only turned to wood),

the body rearing towards the sky's grey murkiness,
charging through corridors and passageways
in frantic ecstasy.
(Small grains of metal scattered by the mane):
We're far now, far past the abyss.

I roar and race, I demand
the fairest of princesses,
in order to...dishonour and devour her
with bloodiest tenderness, and all I see
is those hooves, hooves,
hooves towering over
a naked body.

Only thus can I forget,
though I don't rightly know
what.

The Minotaur on love

The love of the Centaurs is eternal
like being broken on the wheel.

That night, however, when Ariadne
gave Theseus that fateful thread
(and I could see them, for the labyrinth's walls
recede and open at the equinox)
(and I could see them, for I was Theseus
just as Theseus
can be me)
that night they faced each other
and his hands rested
upon her shoulders:

their features were dark
as the waves of the Styx and
their bodies were of stone.
They stood and up above them stood the moon
and stood the sea.
And it was clear that love is not
in movements but
in a kind of menacing
endurance that escapes from time.

At length they turned transparent and
the worms could be seen gnawing
deep within them: she knew then
that she would die on Naxos
and queue for olives as if that
were the meaning of life,
he knew that he would die in Athens,
a king of the theatre
with ten mistresses
and cirrhosis of the liver.

But then they stood, his hands upon her shoulders,
and up above them stood the moon
and there stood the sea. And I,
faced with that love,

I dug my bull's head
into the sand and in some unfamiliar
despair I smashed the walls
and roared O Theseus, Theseus,
I'm waiting for you, Theseus,
and then the labyrinth flung back at me the words
and my own
Homeric laughter.

On Sisyphus

Unable to roll up that boulder,
that boulder or whatever it was, maybe gneiss, maybe paper,
I decided the fault lay with me.
The important thing about faults is they can be corrected,
my mother used to say.

I decided the fault lay with me.
So I added to the boulder
as much weight again. Whatever it was,
maybe hate, maybe love.
And at once it went better. Because

of the certainty that it would
probably break my neck.

Then came the tea-break.
And I realised
that hysteria doesn't solve anything.

On Daedalus

Daedalus potters in the labyrinth.
Self-generating walls.
There's no escape.
Except wings.

And all round – those Icaruses. Swarms of them.
In the towns, in the plains, on the uplands.
In the airport lounge (automatic
goodbyes);
at the space control centre (transistorised
metempsychosis);
on the sports ground (enrolment of pupils
born 1970);
in the museum (blond seepage
of beards);
on the ceiling (a rainbow stain
of imagination);
in the swamps (hooting of night,
born 1640);
in the stone (Pleistocene finger
pointing upward).

Time full of Icaruses,
air full of Icaruses,
spirit full of Icaruses.

Ten billion Icaruses
minus one.

And that even before
Daedalus invented
those wings.

The philosophy of autumn

The late sun's rays
with gentle fingers touch the yellow leaves
outside. Reflected in the window are
a book and a silhouette and a
silhouette, a halo of fair hair;
we are this year
permeated with history
as a cobweb with light.

I ask myself if the prevailing
shortage of geniuses
may not be caused by the disappearance
of tertiary stages of syphilis.

Some kind of heavenly spider
rises above you, above me
and above the aspirin.

The old people's garden

Malignant growth of ivy.
And unkempt grass,
because it no longer matters.
Beneath the trees an invasion
of fruitful Gothic.
Dusk had fallen, mythological
and toothless.

But the Minotaur beat it
through a hole in the fence.
The Icaruses were caught
somewhere in spiders' webs.

In the dawn's early light
the disrespectfully grey, insolent
frontal bone of fact
is revealed.
And it yawns without word.

Whaling

There is a serious shortage of whales.
And yet, in some towns,
whaling flotillas drive along the streets,
so big that the water is too small for them,
or at least a harpoon sneaks
from pavement to pavement,
searching.
It finds.
The house is stuck. A creature elementally
thrashes about and the blood diffuses
in the sky's white eye.

And that is the Old Testament incident,
the primal drama,
the basic event,
to be harpooned and dragged away,
between seaweed and cod,
    between primers and copy-books,
between algae and trawl nets,
    between mugs and mother's photographs,
between slippers and cobwebs in the corner,
between the ship's keel and the sea's keel,
    between the morning and the evening hour,
harpooned and dragged away for the greater glory
of the gods of harpooning and dragging away,
harpooned and dragged away to eternity
to the stifling inwards roar of blood
which tries to resist and with frantic claws
hangs on to the drops from the water tap,
to the reflections on the window pane,
to the first childish hairs
and fins.

Yet there's nothing left but waves and waves
and quartering
on that anonymous other shore,
where there is neither good nor evil,
only the scraping of elastic bone,
the peeling-off of plaster, revealing

older and older medieval frescoes,
the stripping of the skin, revealing
the sliminess of a foetus just conceived.

And now the whistle's painful unison sounds,
the whalers' music,
the fugue which towers in one spot
like an obelisk of a last breath
behind the curtain.

No one has written
that whales' Antigone, the whales' Electra,
the Hamlet of the whales or their Godot,
the whales' Snow White, or even
One Flew over the Whales' Nest,

although the whale is itself
a kind of metaphor.

Metaphors face extinction
in a situation which itself is a metaphor.
And the whales are facing extinction
in a situation which itself is a killer whale.

Homer

Seven cities contend to have harboured his cradle:
Smyrna, Chios, Kollophon,
Ithaké, Pylos, Argos,
Athénai.

Like a lamb he strolls
through marine pastures,
unseen, unburied,
unexcavated, casting no
biographical shadow.

Did he never have trouble with the authorities?
Did he never get drunk? Was he never bugged,
not even when singing?
Did he never love fox terriers, cats,
or young boys?

How much better the Iliad would be
if Agamemnon could be proved to bear
his features or if Helen's biology
reflected contemporary facts.

How much better the Odyssey would be
if he had two heads,
one leg,
or shared one woman
with his publisher.

Somehow he neglected all that
in his blindness.
And thus he towers
in literary history
as a cautionary example
of an author so unsuccessful
that maybe he didn't exist at all.

On the origin of football

A small pebble embedded in concrete:
a statue to the genius of earthworms,
not budging at all.

A small milestone of history,
such a tiny little
triumphal arch
where nothing has ever happened:
not budging at all.

A small rheumatic post
from which someone has stolen the notice
forbidding the stealing of notices:
not budging at all.

An electrified wire
barbedly garrisoning
the dreams of shin ulcers:
not budging at all.

And so, when one day someone encounters
something that's rolling
he kicks it.

And his heavens reverberate,
the temple curtain is rent,
the unrinsed mouths of thousands open wide
in a stifling explosion of silence

like trilobites
yelling *Goal!*

On the origin of 6pm

*Human fates are
simplified by names.*

The day, gnawed by the sun,
tossed among the dummy houses:
we walk, dragging our love behind us
like a big croaked dog.
>   But how many lives have been saved
>   by mouth-to-mouth resuscitation?

And that is all, that vacuum-sealed vanity?
That talk of herrings in an undated tin?
Certainly. And we hold our fork
in the left hand and put the bones
on the side of the plate, for eternity.
>   Your eyes, of course, are neon
>   and wherever you look a fiery
>   writing appears on the wall.

There are no words. There never were
when it came to the crunch. On the threshold of fate
poetry is silent, choked
by its own bitterness.
>   Fortunately I hardly ever
>   understand you.

We write upon each other with scalpels,
like a Chinese poet drawing with a brush.
Some blood coagulates quickly,
some flows and flows.
>   The magnitude of things
>   is measured by the depth of the cut.

We cross on the red light. Because the game
is without rules, and many years ago
they plundered our chessboard squares,
so nothing but the snoring of the kings remains,
and shouts of pawns and neighing of knight's horses:
and on all these we are enjoined to silence.

But when I kiss you
your tongue tastes
of a tenth planet, a parthenogenetic one.

And that is all, that claw of darkness?
These suicides of sleep, from which
we awake right under the stone?
And that is all, that examination
of skeletal remains?
Your gait indeed is royal:
frightening infallibility of breasts.
You walk without motion.

We live by hope. Certainly. Its
parasites gnaw in the brain's emulsion.
A latent image is left.
Sometimes not even that.

And so it's six o'clock
this day. The same as yesterday.
The same as tomorrow.

At home

At home we register the existence of a pernicious rampant growth, of lethal mutations or self-destructive diseases in the body of the world without uneasiness or vertigo. Home is a place of immunity provided that everyone has changed into slippers in the hall and that the gravy contains the customary amount of cornflour.

Home is a state in which the photograph album is a source of immortality and the image in the mirror persists without limit, like a butterfly in a beam of light.

Home is a semi-lethal mutation of the world with the emphasis on the prefix semi-.

Dinner

That soup's to be eaten up to the last spoonful because that's where all the goodness is.

Eat up that lovely soup, don't mess about with it!

Else you'll be weak and won't grow up.

And that'll be your fault.

Just as it is the fault of towns and nations that they've stayed small.

I blame the small nations for not having become powerful. So much the worse for them.

Ich beschuldige die kleinen Nationen...

Accuso le piccole nazioni...

J'accuse les petites nations...

Come on, get that soup down before it's like ice!

A philosophy of encounters

A train which is the mirror image of another train. A handshake from window to window. A cordial talk between very close people in windows moving parallel away from each other.

– Next time –

– Yes, next time –

– Next time we meet –

– Yes, next time we'll meet next time.

Whereby next time means last time and last time is last time only because it could be next time.

Every process in nature can, under the same law, unroll also in reverse: the principle of parity.

Of course the principle of parity does not apply to weak interactions.

Elsewhere

A journey, like changing from one rib-cage
into another, air pressure pressing from above
and below, we contract,
we're in the capillaries, barely capable of
the main stream, hidden, vainly
sought by the news and vainly seeking,

embryos trembling with the breath
of non-existing Fates.

After a while the mollusc in us
pushes out its shapeless head; it is waiting for
the postman
with a white letter
with the definition of fog,
known also as the natural state of affairs.

The postman comes. He has green eyes,
a bag containing kisses on the forehead,
some fingerprints
and registered mail.

The postman passes by and calls nextdoor.
Gently and calmly
a tornado rises.

We are flooded out
we are exposed

and we left
our brolly
at home.

On the origin of the contrary

Like the sky breaking up –
but it was only a pair of hands.

For a while it beat its wings
but the hands closed
even more. The wings resisted.
It scraped its feet but the hands
closed and one leg broke off.

Each time it moved something
the hands closed and something broke off.
So it kept rigid. It might have been
catalepsy.

But it might have been a creeping realisation
that there's no longer any blue.
                          On the contrary.
That there's no longer a meadow with flowers
here and there.
                  On the contrary.
That there's neither glucose
              nor rustling
              nor time
                      but on the contrary.

And that's how things stand. Until
someone gets tired of it. This life,
this death, or that tickle on the palm.

On the origin of memory

The day dawns over the sea.
The polyps are singing.
But what remains are
old and new
assuredly lacerating
coral reefs.

Song is and is not.

But what remains
after all that bleeding?

A hermetic theory
of the blood clot.

On the origin of full power

This time,
when houses sit on eggs
of a small Easter death
and a symphony orchestra lies
in ambush under the bushes,

when drums and trombones
pounce on people in the park,
demanding alms in excess of
live body weight,

he listens to a no longer familiar
internal unison,
to his storm in a teacup,
to his And yet and yet,

from the quick little flame
he does not recognise the big city,
he realises the weariness of the mountain mass
face to face with a falling stone

and this time at least
when asked replies:

Yes, I can.

And he goes his way
of the flute.

Conversation with a poet

Are you a poet?
    Yes, I am.
How do you know?
    I've written poems.
If you've written poems it means you *were* a poet. But now?
    I'll write a poem again one day.
In that case maybe you'll be a poet again one day. But how will you
know it is a poem?
    It will be a poem just like the last one.
Then of course it won't be a poem. A poem is only once and can
never be the same a second time.
    I believe it will be just as good.
How can you be sure? Even the quality of a poem is for once only
and depends not on you but on circumstances.
    I believe that circumstances will be the same too.
If you believe that then you won't be a poet and never were a poet.
What makes you think you are a poet?
    Well – I don't rightly know. And who are you?

INTERFERON, OR ON THEATRE

INTERFERON, ČILI O DIVADLE
(1986)

TRANSLATED BY EWALD OSERS
WITH ADDITIONAL TRANSLATIONS
BY DAVID YOUNG & DANA HÁBOVÁ
AND IAN & JARMILA MILNER

The soul

In Queen's Street
on Friday night
– lights only just blossoming
but already with the pomegranates
of shows for adults only –
among the herds of cars
a yellow
inflatable balloon
was bouncing about
with what remained of its helium soul,
still two lives left,

amidst the song of armour
bouncing with yellow
balloon fright
in front of wheels
and behind wheels,

incapable of salvation and
incapable of destruction,
one life left,
half a life left,
just a molecular trace of helium,

and with its last ounce of strength
searching with its string
for a small child's hands
on Sunday morning.

[EO]

Burning

The fire was creeping along the logs,
whispering curses and incantations.
Then it settled in a corner
and began to grow and to sing.
It found its language
in an old letter
from mother.

Orestes' fire. Antigone's fire.
The terrible fire: it is hot
and the smoke rises to heaven.

[EO]

Sunday

The Marathon runners have reached the turning point:
Sunday, that day of sad songs
by the railway bridge
and the clouds.
                Your eyes, at zenith –
and to say this without using the body is
like running without touching the ground.

                Thirty years ago
a transport passed here, open wagons
loaded with silhouettes,
with heads and shoulders cut out
from the black paper of horror.
And these people loved somebody,
but the train returns empty
every Sunday, only
a few hairgrips
and cinders
on the wagon floor.

Who knows how to touch the ground,
who knows how not to touch the ground?

No choice but to believe
in the existence of the Marathon's finishing line
in two hours and forty minutes,
amidst the deafening din of the clouds
and of empty open wagons
on the railway bridge.

[EO]

196

United Flight 1011

Megalopolis far behind,
engulfed by air. Remaining only
a few towers, the din of millions,
the shells on Coney Island beach
and the gentle yielding of your body
in the atmospheric disturbance
called morning.

Thirty thousand feet up
you answered: Yes,
I love you, yes.
Then the sign came up to
Fasten Seat Belts and the B-737
set down for a smooth landing.

Basically, of course, it remained fixed
in the vast white box of the sky
like a butterfly on the pin of a word.

For where would we be
if love were not stronger than poetry
and poetry stronger than love?

[EO]

Dreams

They sap man's substance
as moon the dew.
A rope grows erect
from the crown of the head.
A black swan hatches
from a pebble.
And a flock of angels in the sky
is taking an evening class
on the skid pan.

I dream, so I dream.
I dream
that three times three is nine,
that the right-hand
rule applies;
and when the circus leaves
the trampled ground will
once more overgrow with grass.

Yes, grass.
Unequivocal grass.
Just grass.

[EO]

198

The last night bus

The last bus echoes away
in the depth
of night's
spinal canal.

The stars tremble
unless they explode.

There are no other civilisations.
Only a gentle
galactic fear
on a methane base.

[EO]

A lecture on arthropods

The mite Adactylidium
hatches in his mother's body,
eats up his mother's body from inside
while mating
with all his seven
little sisters.

So that when he's born
it's just as if he had died:
he's been through it all

and is freelancing now
in the target's bull's-eye,
at the focus of non-obligatory existence:

an absolute poet,
non-segmented,
non-antenniferous,
eight-legged.

[EO]

Immanuel Kant

The philosophy of white blood cells:
this is self,
this is non-self.
The starry sky of non-self
perfectly mirrored
deep inside.
Immanuel Kant
perfectly mirrored
deep inside.

And he knows nothing about it,
is only afraid of draughts.
And he knows nothing about it,
though just this is the critique
of pure reason.

Deep inside.

[EO]

Biodrama

The puppet king
stages a mounted hunt
for sausages.
Terrified boiling wursts
and bewildered frankfurters
scuttle through thickets,
their fat little bellies
pierced by arrows.

They are close to extinction.
The last specimens
are kept
in refrigerated cages
at the Babylon zoo.

The balance of nature
has again been upset. The knell
has been sounded for the invertebrates.

A few foolish children
are crying.

[EO]

Distant howling

In Alsace,
on 6th July 1885,
a rabid dog knocked down
the nine-year-old Joseph Meister
and bit him fourteen times.

Meister was the first patient
saved by Pasteur
with his vaccine, in thirteen
progressive doses
of the attenuated virus.

Pasteur died of ictus
ten years later.
The janitor Meister
fifty-five years later
committed suicide
when the Germans occupied
his Pasteur Institute
with all those poor dogs.

Only the virus
remained above it all.

[EO]

Jewish cemetery at Olšany,
Kafka's grave, April, a sunny day

Searching under the sycamores
are some words poured out from language.
Loneliness skin-tight
and therefore stony.

The old man by the gate,
looking like Gregor Samsa
but unmetamorphosed,
squints in this
naked light
and answers every question:

I'm sorry, I don't know.
I'm a stranger here.

[EO]

When the bees fell silent

An old man
suddenly died
alone in his garden under an elderberry bush.
He lay there till dark,
when the bees
fell silent.

A lovely way to die, wasn't it,
doctor, says
the woman in black
who comes to the garden
as before,
every Saturday,

in her bag always
lunch for two.

[EO]

The dead

After his third operation, his heart
riddled like an old fairground target,
he woke up on his bed
and said: Now I'll be fine,
fit as a fiddle. And have you ever seen
horses coupling?

He died that night.

And another dragged on through eight insipid years
like a river weed in an acid stream,
as if pushing up his pallid
skewered face over the cemetery wall.

Until that face eventually vanished.

Both here and there the angel of death
quite simply stamped his hobnailed boot
on their medulla oblongata.

I know they died the same way.
But I don't believe that they are
dead the same way.

[EO]

206

Half a hedgehog

The rear half had been run over,
leaving the head and thorax
and the front legs of the hedgehog shape.

A scream from a cramped-open
jaw. The scream of the mute is
more horrible than the silence after a flood,
when even black swans float
belly upwards.

And even if some hedgehog doctor were
to be found in a hollow trunk or under the leaves
in a beechwood there'd be no hope
for that mere half on Road E12.

In the name of logic,
in the name of the theory of pain,
in the name of the hedgehog god the father, the son
and the holy ghost amen,
in the name of games and unripe raspberries,
in the name of tumbling streams of love
ever different and ever bloody,
in the name of the roots which overgrow
the heads of aborted foetuses,
in the name of satanic beauty,
in the name of skin bearing human likeness,
in the name of all halves
and double helices, of purines
and pyrimidines

we tried to run over
the hedgehog's head with the front wheel.

And it was like guiding a lunar module
from a planetary distance,
from a control centre seized
by cataleptic sleep.

And the mission failed. I got out
and found a heavy piece of brick.
Half the hedgehog continued screaming. And now
the scream turned into speech,

prepared by
the vaults of our tombs:
Then death will come and it will have your eyes.

[EO]

Interferon

Always just one demon in the attic.
Always just one death in the village. And the dogs
howling in that direction. And from the other end
the new-born child arrives, the only one
to fill the empty space in that wide air.

Likewise also cells infected by a virus
send out a signal all around them and defences
are mobilised so that no other virus
has any hope just then of taking root
or changing fate. This phenomenon
is known as interference.

And when a poet dies in the depth of night
a single black bird wakens in the thicket
and sings for all it is worth
while from the sky a black rain trickles down
like sperm or something,
the song is spattered and the choking bird
sings sitting on an empty rib-cage
in which an imaginary heart
awakes to its forever interfering
futility. And in the morning the sky is clear,
the bird is weary and the soil is fertilised.
The poet is no more.

In Klatovy Street, in Pilsen,
by the railway bridge, there was
a shop with quilted bedcovers.
In times when there's a greater need
for a steel cover over our continent
business in quilted bedcovers
is slack. The shopkeeper was hard up.
Practical men when hard up usually
turn to art.
In his shopwindow, open to the interior
of his shop, its owner built
a gingerbread house of quilts
and every evening staged

a performance about a quilted
gingerbread house and a red-quilted
Little Red Riding Hood, while his wife
in this quilted masquerade was alternately
the wolf or the witch, and he himself
a padded-out Hansel,
or Gretel, Red Riding Hood or grandmother.
The sight of the two old people
crawling about in swollen billows
of textiles round the chubby cottage
was not unambiguous. It was a little like
the life of sea cucumbers in the mud
under a reef. Outside thundered
the approaching surf of war and they
conducted their quilted
pantomime outside time and action.

For a while children would stand outside but
soon they would go home. Nothing was sold.
But it was the only pantomime
at that time. The black bird sang
and rain poured into a rib-cage
wearing the Star of David.

But in the actors under those quilted covers
l'anima allegra must have just then awoken
and so, sweating and rapt, they acted
their undersea *commedia dell'arte*,
thinking there was a backstage until
a scene was finished, jerkily they moved
from shopwindow to gingerbread house and back,
with the exuberance of Columbines
stricken by polio, while the music
of fifes and drums did not reach them.

Or else they thought that such a deep
humiliation of the customary dignity of age
interfered with the steps of gentlemen
in leather coats and with
the departure of trains to human slaughterhouses.
It did.

The black bird sang and the ruined
sclerotic hearts leapt in their breasts,
and then one morning when they didn't play
and had not even raised the blind –
the sky was clear, the soil was fertilised –
the quilted bedcovers were confiscated
for the eastern front and the actors
transferred to the backstage
of the world, called Bergen-Belsen.
No trace is left of the shop today:
it's now a greengrocer's with woody parsnips.

Always just one death in the village.
Always just one demon.
Great is the power of the theatre, even if
it always does get knocked down in the end
and flung backstage.

The dogs howl in that direction.
And the butterfly pursues the man
who stole the flowers.

When we did autopsies at the psychiatric
hospital in Bohnice, filled with the
urban exudations of relative futility,
the car would tip us out amidst the ward blocks
whose inmates waved from windows
with some kind of May Day pennants, and then
one went, hugely alone,
beyond a spinney to the solitary morgue, where
the naked bodies of ancient schizophrenics
awaited us, along with two live inmates; one of them
would pull the corpses up from underground
with a rope hoist and place them
upon the tables as a mother might an infant
for baptism, while the other was lurking, pen ready poised,
in a dark corner to write up
the Latin protocol, and he wrote faultlessly.
Neither of them uttered the slightest sound, only
the hoist shaft moaned...and the knife
drawn over skin and dermis made a sound
of satin tearing...and they were always

enormous and unprecedented pneumonias
and tumours as big as dragons' eggs,
it rained into the opened thorax –
and in that roaring silence one had to
break the line of an angel's fall
and dictate the logical verdict
on a long-sentenced demon...
and the schizophrenic's pen in the corner
busily scraped across the paper
like an eager mouse.

We need no prompters
said the puppets haughtily.

The air of that anatomical theatre
was filled with interferon,
it was a great personal demonstration
against malignant growth, it was
a general amnesty for the walls, entropy
was abjured for the moment

because there are no bubbles at the bottom
to burst under the breeze.

The red balloon outside rose up
to an unsuspected sky, its chains
strained by the certainty that the nearer the inferno
the greater the paradise,
the nearer the prison cell
the greater the freedom.
Cantabit vacuus coram latrone viator.

And that is the weird essence of the theatre
that an actor stripped of everything mounts to
the very top of the conflagration
and everything else dies down, falls silent
like a long-hunted animal, its muscles
still twitching but with endorphines
and an infinite peace in the brain.

Yes, even a whale will sometimes leave the school,
hurl itself into shallow water and perish in the sun

like a levelled cathedral, with pushed-out penis,
and death is instantly buried
in a grain of sand
and the sea laughs.

Go ask the tree-stumps; in broken language
they preach about saplings. And in the jargon
of galactic white dwarfs the stars
of the main sequence shine forever.

In the non-Euclidean curved space,
which eludes understanding as much as
the interference of the theatre,
you ceaselessly hear the voices of children
from the primary school of death,
children from the puppet tragedies of the kitchen
and children from the junketings of war,
when skewering them on lances
with their wriggling little legs
provided spice like curry for the mercenaries,
voices of children eluding understanding –

But we've washed behind our ears,
we've stopped pulling the cat's tail,
we've stopped shoving our fingers
into electric sockets –

What else is there left in the universe
of hominisation, slow as the decay of tritium,
than the doctrine of the growing sense of shame of demons:
since Aztec times high priests no longer
offer up sacrifice while dressed in the skin
of a freshly flayed prisoner.

We need no prompters, they said –

Once on St Nicholas' Day, the man acting the Devil,
dead drunk, fell down some stairs and lay there,
and a child, experiencing that embarrassing
joy mere inches from terror,
ran out after the thump and called:

Mummy, come here, there's a dead devil –

And so he was, even though the actor
picked himself up after another tot. Maybe the dogs howled,
but only by a black mistake.
In the sky shone the stars of the main sequence,
the bird was getting ready in the thicket,
the child shivered a little
from the chill of three million years,
in that wide air, but
they prompted him, poetically,

you're only imagining all this,
look, the butterfly's already
bringing the flowers back...and
there's no other devil left...and
the nearer paradise...

He believed, and yet he didn't.

[EO]

214

Collision

To think I might have been dead,
he said to himself, ashamed, as if this were
a curse of the heart, raising a bundle of bones
to a man's height. As if it were suddenly
forbidden to touch even words that had dropped to the ground.
Besides, he was afraid of finding
his body in a metal press. Embarrassing
down to the capillaries.

The tram stood jammed above him
like an icebreaker's prow and all that was left of the car
was a grotesque pretzel with a chunk bitten off
by the dentures of a demented angel.
Something dark was dripping on the rails,
and a strikingly pale wind was leafing
through a book still warm.

People were forming a circle and with deaf-mute
sympathy awaited the play's catharsis,
like maggots emerging from
under the wings of a beheaded chicken.
From afar came the approaching wail of sirens,
congealing in the jinxed air-conditioning of that day
and that minute. Dewdrops were falling
on the back of the neck like remnants of
atmospheric dignity. Embarrassing down to the capillaries.

No, thank you, he said, I'll wait;
for a silent film had started to run
without subtitles, without colour and without answers.

And what about the magnetic monopoles
escaping seconds after the Big Bang,
protons violating the irreversibility of the flow of time?

What about the giant molecular clouds
under the galaxy's shoulders, conceiving
the embryos of stars?

What about the loneliness of the first genes
accumulating amino acids in shallow primeval pools
at the expense of entropic usurers?

What about the desiccated starfish
like proto-eagles' talons dug into the bed
of a vanishing sea?

What about the mortal migrations of birds
observing the sun's inclination
and the roar of sex-hormones?

What about the caged half-crazed
orang-utan who vomits because
he has nothing else to do?

What about the mice which for a thousand years
have learned to sing and the frogs balancing
on one leg like the thigh
of a beauty queen from Mesopotamia?

What about poetry, an enterprise
so disorderly it twists the rulers
and increases the squint of school inspectors?

And what about the little girl
in the leukemia ward who, on the toilet,
tried to show what kind of moustache the kind doctor has,
but as her skinny sticks of hands let go of
the edge of the bowl she falls in and so
tried again and again?

And what about the weak-kneed intellectual,
the professor who understood the approximate universe
but forgot the traffic rules?

No, thank you, he said to some uniform,
I don't need anything. My papers are in my pocket
but I can't reach there. And he tried
to smile a little at this embarrassment of completed creation.
It's all my fault, he said,
thank you.
                    And then he died.

Landscapes

Yes, you were there. We were supposed to lift beets but the totally
drunk engineer kept throwing them straight at us so that we had to
dodge them. And he kept inviting you to have a schnapps with him.
Morass mixed with hate. The photographer fell into the stream and
was badly bruised. An ambulance was on its way.

But in the distance all was peaceful.
Far to the north, up on the plateau
fine smoke. Somebody roasting somebody.

Far to the west
a gathering of hunters, fat
as opossums. Their jaws

were masticating every kind of mammal
and bird, as if to choke the balance of the sky.

Far to the south grey clouds
were copulating and a bolt of lightning
was stuck in the clay,
shaped like a tree.

Then came the farm officials and began to curse because the beet
was all over the place. As everybody else was drunk they berated us.

On the field-path by the mouse-hole
bloomed a butterbur confused by
this spectacle of autumn,
although it was all
perfectly obvious.

[EO]

217

Memo to a pre-school-age daughter

When no one's watching
behind us
the sky and the rain are rolled up
like music paper with a trumpet part,
houses and squares are tidied away in a box
padded with newspapers,
the birds change into letters
in a secret black book,
puddles reflecting night and distant
fires are stowed away in the attic
like grandfather's presents to grandmother.

The trams are put away in cotton-wool clouds.
Pedestrians go to the cloakrooms
and unwrap their sandwiches:
their walking is over
when no one's watching.
And through the city, on seven long legs
a giant spider stalks and in a whisper
advertises the next scene.

It's interval time in the dubious theatre
of a thousand actors and one spectator.

When you're elsewhere the home left behind
shrinks to a blown-glass crib
under a superannuated Christmas tree.
Dogs with eyes like teacups
and dogs with eyes like millstones
carry off your princess
from the gloomy castle, where
philosophers stand on their heads
and the king puts away his crown,
too heavy for a fool.

Flocks of other children rise
into the branches of the ancient elm
and twitter as they fall asleep.

When you're elsewhere the home behind
is soaked up into a small mirror
and our parents act in a theatre of flies
of which you're unaware because it is
a play within a play
and night's about to fall.

That's why I always cried a little
when we had detention
and home was not in sight.

But now I have got used to it.

Even though
I still don't know the play.

[EO]

The man who wants to be himself

He flings out the plastic flowers and chases away the electric current. He sweeps out all voices and shadows and with two turns of a major key locks them out. Two days and two nights he showers in the dew. He takes an eraser and rubs out all traces of non-self on his self. His skin is now as pink as an embryonic membrane and his soul is lighter than helium.

He floats up over his garden, a toadstool cap on his head and fossil foliage on his shoulders. He collects the teeth of extinct species and places them under his tongue.

Now he is himself, he whispers to himself in the unknown language of the Aztecs.

He extends his hand to shake it, but the hand itself refuses.

He searches for himself under the stones but he just cannot find himself. Not on the bottom, not on the surface, not in the washbasin, not in the mirror and not under the carpet.

I'm probably not worthy of myself, the man mutters.

Perhaps I'd better not admit I'm me.

[EO]

A well-read man
or A meeting with Russell Edson

A certain man enters a bookshop because he has decided to stand up to the voraciousness of books. He picks up a book from a stand, looks around, and shakes out the letters. Then he picks up another book and another, and shakes out the letters. Surreptitiously he kicks the little black heap of letters under a bookcase.

He continues, row after row, leaving on the shelves the empty hides of the bound books and the deflated bellies of paperbacks. His eyes shine and his spirit touches the paper stars on the ceiling. He no longer picks and chooses.

But then he comes up against a book with sticky letters. People today are terribly cunning. The letters stick to his hands, they get up his sleeves, they tickle him under his ribs, they crawl over his face. In front he is covered with writing like a page from a newspaper. An initial clings to his flies, the print-run figure sticks to his shoe. He tiptoes behind the stand and brushes himself down. It's no use – the more he brushes himself down, the more letters crawl over him, the more he pats himself the more letters appear because – as might have been expected – suitably matched sticky letters mate when they are agitated and instantly produce young.

How is the lettered man going to get out of the shop?

The lettered man walks up to the pay desk and declares that this is his book, that he himself has written it all over himself. All the remaining books burst out laughing and the man leaves after a payment for overheads and author's tax. But there's no way of getting home. Lettered citizens are not allowed on any public transport, for who the hell can tell what the text means or what's hidden behind it?

So the lettered man makes his way home on foot, through side streets, and the children spell him out.

When he reaches home he is very tired: literature is no lightweight affair. He wants to lie down. But his wife chases him out of the bedroom because letters are crawling out of him like fleas from a dead dog. The wife gets out the hoover and the man beats himself on the carpet rack. You aren't coming indoors like that, says the wife. The man wants to go into the dog kennel but his wife won't let him do that either because the dog might catch the mange from the letters. The man takes some candles, goes down to the cellar and reads himself. And don't you dare come upstairs, his wife calls down to him, till you've read yourself absolutely clean.

The man reads and reads, and his wife is getting the dinner ready from a few steamed poems.

[EO]

A lecture on diseases

Diseases of puppets are tiny, thread-like, with soft funereal furcoats and big ears. And small claw-like feet.

There is no fever. Only the sawdust trickling from their sleeves.

Diarrhoea only like woe from wit.

Cardiac arhythmia only like the tick of the death-watch beetle.

It doesn't even look like disease. More like attentive listening, falling over one's eyes like a hood.

When the strings break, that's the end. All that's left is a wooden peg on the banks of Lethe. And at the crossing the little green man comes on: Walk!

Chin up, calls the puppeteer. We'll do Macbeth, calls the puppeteer. Everyone kicks the bucket in that play anyway. And the remaining puppets obediently line up backstage and tip the water out of their little boots.

[EO]

Swans in flight

It's like violence done to the atmosphere; as if Michelangelo reached out from the stone. And all the swans on the entire continent always take off together, for they are linked by a single signalling circuit. They are circling, and that means that Fortinbras's army is approaching. That Hamlet will be saved and that an extra act will be played. In all translations, in all theatres, behind all curtains and without mercy.

The actors are already growing wings against fate.

Hold out – that's all.

[EO]

Teeth

Teeth are rather ridiculous remains of the outside inside. Their life is filled with dread that they might find themselves on the outside again and get lost there. A lost tooth doesn't know which way to turn, it doesn't know whether it is clenched or revealed in a smile, it doesn't know how to strike root and thus lose its capacity for aching.

A lot of teeth have been lost during the evolution of civilisations. Either through educational or corrective interventions in the lives of young individuals, or through decay in old age. Teeth knocked out during the evolution of civilisations and cultures do not rot but trudge through subterranean darkness, afraid to come out into the light. Teeth wearied by their pilgrimage are discovered, thus causing a number of new scientific disciplines to emerge.

The remaining teeth get together on cloud-darkened evenings, trembling with fright and exchanging stories of gums, fists, jackboots and other stomatological implements. These stories are not devoid of a certain unintentional comic element. The teeth become comic figures and repeat their stories night after night, century after century.

That's how the puppet theatre began.

It is a theatre of teeth for which no mouths were left.

So close your mouths, dear children, and pay attention.

[EO]

The cast

Punch   (pink costume with jingle bells, especially on his cap; about two feet tall, more or less sexless and lacking adrenal glands; expert on good and evil)

Johnny   (country bumpkin, transparent as a fresh spring, member of the local gymnastic club; helps old ladies across the state highway and collects wild berries and waste paper)

The Princess   (brocade and a tiara of genuine cheap costume jewellery, speaks foreign languages as well as the speech of the common people; she is post-pubertal but still waiting for her dragon)

The Dragon   (genus Agamidae, with many spare parts, well-preserved)

The Water-Sprite Michael   (green, frog-like, freshwater but has often found himself at sea, hence his bronchial and respiratory catarrh)

Little Red Riding Hood   (red cap on fair hair, parents in steady jobs, grandmother an alcoholic)

The Witch   (used to be Little Red Riding Hood herself, she has warts and a burlap bundle; readily multiplies into groups of two to four; fries only with honest-to-goodness fat)

Old Man Škrhola   (rugged but simple-minded, which enables him to have a clear-cut opinion on everything; dressed in a subfusc coat and a sheepskin hat because a man should keep his head out of the wind)

Old Dame Škrhola   (knows her name and address, wears plain national costume; regarded as an expert on the biographies of all the other puppets)

The Sorcerer Gruntorád   (pointed hat and a yellow eye; his cave is in such a mess that minor miracles occur spontaneously)

Doctor Faustus   (full beard to hide a neurotic mouth-twitch; his poodle has already caught it from him)

Matýsek the Cop   (white tunic, blue straps supporting his drum and drumsticks; huge shako with a peak, does not acknowledge civvies; mostly invents his decrees)

Marguerite   (poor thing)

The King   (a king)

Knights, devils and others.

[EO]

The beginnings of the puppet theatre

Originally, in newborn and toddler times,
Punch, the size of a near-adult lemur,
would scamper through the meadows, herding his building blocks
and singing dirty songs.
The King ruled over climbing ivy and
the Dragon, bastard son of infusoria and runes,
splashed happily about in a drop of water.

The molecular weight of the Princess was
about 200,000.
Then the sun rose and shadows were cast.
Through natural selection among the shadows
the puppeteer evolved. The puppeteer
decided that it was improper for Punch
to sing dirty songs, for kings to rule over ivy,
for love to be made in drops of water or for
the molecular weight of beautiful women to be measured.
He decided that the proper course would be
for everything to have its line and spine. And so
Punch and the King, the Dragon and the Princess
all had a wire pushed through the tops of their heads,
a long way down.

The massive mess of promiscuous primal procreation
was replaced by the orderliness of dim reason.
Thus Punch turned mute, the King turned idiotic,
the Dragon turned to stone, the Princess miscarried,
and the building blocks scampered all over the world.

And all was silent, void and motionless as
in a museum of hunting trophies.
It was nothing to do with the theatre. Not even
an occasion for folklore.
So the puppeteer fitted strings to the fossils'
hands and feet, so they could be comically jerked,
giving rise to new life. The puppets could grin,
mouths open ear to ear,
multiplied by carving the soft wood,
uttering words of wisdom cribbed by classical authors

from other classical authors.

And the ivy grows and grows, from liver to brain,
from cradle to altar, up the curtain and
down again,

to the effective applause of children who
have never heard of silence and have forgotten
the piercing roar of primal creation.

[EO]

Punch, the Princess, Johnny and other children watch the cheerful play of the kittens

A velvet paw but a sparkling eye.
Eh bien, n'y touchez pas…?
Boundless the world of play,
a huge crystal ball
containing the two
(kittens),
dark-gleaming,
milk-tender,
rambling roses
born of a flute,
anxiously seeking the warmth of hands,
writing the world's soft side with little claws,

these two
and a dancing mouse,
whose throat they've bitten through,
still twitching skinny feet.
Tout de même, ils sont comme nous.

[EO]

230

Sir Rudolph, the knight

He won the femur fencing bout,
He won the belfry toss, spot on.
He won the 5 x 8 metre race.

He won the quail swallowing event
  and the swan riding.
He won the leap across the Rubicon
  with a half-turn.

He won the blood pouring from bucket
  into the storage tank as well as
  the blood count.
He won the sackcloth quick-change.
He won the love-song contest
  and came top in testosterone production.
He won the entombment
  and the resurrection.
He won the victory-count event.

Then a knot dropped out of his cardiac region.
He was glued up again with flour-paste,
  which is the elixir
  of winners.

[EO]

Faustus

Recently
Doctor Faustus
was flung out to the attic.
His performance no longer
satisfactory.

He'd come to believe
he really was Doctor Faustus.

His poodle had croaked.

His apprentice Wagner
delivered the closing speech
and from each word
leapt a hyena.

[EO]

Marguerite

I beseech Thee, Lady of Sorrows, look down on my misery.
I am but love, I know nothing else. The gates of hell
yawn beyond the curtain.
I beseech Thee, Lady of Sorrows,
at our one hundred and sixty-second performance
make Heinrich, that's Faustus, be careful. Let him not sign with his
    blood,
let him marry me, let us make love, let the lights be switched off,
let our children without strings and wires
sing unknown songs, resounding
among the paper treetops.

I know it's only a play.
But only a play is stronger
than damnation.

[EO]

In the box

The Dragon is licking his wounds.
The devils are keeping each other warm.
The Witch has given the Princess a scarf
the poor girl's always cold.
Punch is biting his nails.
Johnny is snoring.
Škrhola is re-counting his salary,
it doesn't add up.

Now and again
one of them furtively
crawls out of the paper,
finds a piece of wire
and blindly searches for somebody's head.

It's no great matter, he'd merely
like to poke someone's eye out,
to have a souvenir
of this season in paradise.

[EO]

Princesses

To trumpet flourishes
and the ringing of bells,
behind drawn curtains
the joyful decapitation
of princesses.

Their bodies are taken
hostage
and their dreams are enacted
independently
on the high ceiling
of the shadow theatre.

And in the morning, naked in the nakedness
of the other person,
we ask ourselves whose hands are these

and from which play came
this immortal scene
from the ancient dynasty
of If.

[EO]

The sorcerer's lament

First it was too wet.
        So there was no spell-casting.
Then the fountains dried up, yeast
aborted, water-snakes turned
into watch-chains and watercolours became
the sand of heavenly tracks.
        So spell-casting wasn't possible.

Some years I completed
my tax return on white mice.
The King had a row with the Queen,
wallpaper grew ears, fire
rolled up into linoleum
and lightning struck the piano.
        So it was impossible to tell
        if there was any spell-casting or not.

Eventually there was a total shortage
of bats. I made them out of paper
but they resembled little flying pigs.
And they were eaten up by the thready tapeworms
from the typewriters. My magic wand
got pregnant by a retired saint.
My apprentices took to the bottle.
        So that, in actual fact, I never
        began spell-casting.

But my great magic is
that I'm still here. A medium-grade
halo over both my heads.

[EO]

236

Punch's dream

I'll slip out in front of the curtain, taking
great care not to tangle my strings
in the flies,
I'll jingle my bells (merrily),
doff my cap
and before the puppeteer knows what's happening
I'll speak in my own voice,
you know,
my own voice,
out of my own head,
for the first and the last time,
because afterwards they'll put me back in the box,
wrapped in tissue paper.
I'll say what I've wanted to say
for a whole eternity of wood,

I'll say it, no matter how ridiculous
my little voice may sound, how embarrassingly squeaky,
I'll say the most important, the most crucial thing,
I'll speak my piece...

Maybe it will be heard.
Maybe someone will take note.
Maybe they won't laugh.
Maybe it'll grow in the children
and irritate the grown-ups.
Maybe it'll change the colour of the set.
Maybe it'll rouse the cardboard
and the spotlights' shadows. Maybe it'll shift
the laws of relativity.

I'll say...Hi there, kids, you're a great bunch,
say hello to your pal Punch!

[EO]

How we played the Gilgamesh epic

Working mainly from the Neo-Assyrian version our puppet-master wrote a play that had no equal in the field of puppet theatre. Our company, he believed, had the right actors for the different characters.

Matýsek the Cop would act the powerful King Gilgamesh. He knows how to handle a drum and drumsticks, which he'll drop, as it were, into the Nether World in Act XII. Enkidu, the hairy forest dweller, will be played by the Devil Marbuel, and the Lady of Easy Virtue, who puts other ideas into Enkidu's head, by the Princess. Dame Škrhola will be perfect as the Goddess Ishtar: she'll just have to shed a few clothes. Utnapishtim, who built the ark for the Flood, will be the sorcerer Gruntorád – without his hat, of course. That leaves us Franz the Footman and Sir Rudolph the Knight for the gods Shamash and Enlil. The only problem we had was with the monsters. So it was decided that Humbaba could be played by old Škrhola wearing the head of the Dragon, and the Bull of Heaven by the rest of the Dragon, whose haunch could be easily unscrewed and flung at the Goddess Ishtar. Hansel and Punch could both undergo a succession of quick changes to enact the remaining goddesses, gods, serpents, wolves, scorpions and the people of Uruk.

To make the play suitable for juvenile audiences the puppeteer deleted all questionable passages, such as Enkidu's fornication with the Lady of Easy Virtue, Gilgamesh's wedding with the Goddess Ishtar, and the ban on sexual intercouse in the city of Uruk. This greatly simplified the action. In the time gained there would be hurdy-gurdy music and the Lady of Easy Virtue would lecture Enkidu on the advantages of a school education.

During rehearsals the puppeteer then decided to leave out also all fights and battles, since their educational value was questionable and they tended to break the puppets' strings. Actually, in the fight between Gilgamesh and Enkidu the Devil Marbuel's nose got damaged, so that his place had to be taken by a hurriedly dug-up Doctor Faustus with Beelzebub's hairy hide stuck on him. These scenes were therefore replaced by geographical lectures given by the Water-Sprite Michael in front of the curtain.

Then it was found that the sets
lacked a cedar forest and the roaring of the Giant Humbaba made
        the puppeteer
lose his voice. The swords
with two-talent blades and their thirty-pound
hilts wielded by both sides
got lost during rehearsals.
The elamak-wood table, the cornelian bowls
filled with honey, the lapis lazuli bowls
filled with butter had not been delivered at all.
To open a trap so that
Enkidu's spirit might waft up from the Nether World,
like a gust of wind, was a technical
impossibility. But the acting was totally dedicated:

Punch and Hansel scamper across the farmyard, yelling:
    Thou hast created Gilgamesh,
    create thou now his likeness.
    Let him stand up to his turbulent heart.
    Let them pit their strength 'gainst each other,
    so that Uruk regain its peace.

In a forest clearing sits hairy Faustus with the Princess,
declaiming:
    I fain would challenge him and boldly speak to him,
    I want to shout in Uruk: I am strong!
    I am the one who changeth destiny!
    I am he that was born in the wilderness, that is blessed with strength!
And the Princess says with feeling:
    Eat bread, Enkidu,
    And drink beer, as is the custom here!

Matýsek the Cop waves his halberd from the ramparts
and hollers:
    I want to turn my hand to the task and fell cedars,
    I want to earn eternal glory!

Then the Water-Sprite Michael talks about forestry management
in Lebanon. And then comes Škrhola with his dragon's head:
    Let me go free, Gilgamesh! Thou shalt be my lord
    and I thy servant. And the trees
    I've grown for thee I now shall cut for thee
    and I will build thee houses from them.

239

No sooner has Škrhola dropped dead decently
than the old dame cries out beneath the lime tree:
    If thou wilt not create the Bull of Heaven
    for me I'll smash the gates of the Nether World, shatter its hinges,
    lead forth the dead
    who will devour the living...
Then Doctor Faustus flings at her the Dragon's haunch
and Franz the Footman is exceedingly irate.

At this the puppeteer is greatly cheered
by all this action and, with ceaseless assurances
that this epic is a huge success,
chases all his puppets across the stage,
at random makes them wave their arms and legs
and in a mighty bass declaims the linking text,
so that Sumerian remnants float about in a verbal deluge;
and as he roars:
    Who is the finest hero of them all,
    who the most splendid of all men?
he kicks over the spotlight of the god Shamash
and through a total chaos ring the verses:
    When he had travelled four times two hours
    the darkness thickened, there's no light,
    he can see nothing, either front or back,
    when he had travelled five times two hours
    the darkness thickened...

and nobody knows who is who,
torn is the curtain, and torn is the cap
of Punch, the children's friend,
and everyone goes home, no one knows where,
and in the box the Water-Sprite Michael, who on stage
escaped the worst,
quietly quotes Enkidu:
    Heaven was calling,
    Earth responded. And I stood all alone –
and then he adds: Blimey, this ain't half powerful,
this epic stuff. And anyway, we'll never
get such good parts again. Never.

[EO]

240

The autumnal bus

With an asthmatic puff the front door opens. Tripping on the steps the Passengers pour inside, collars turned up, weighed down with bags and bundles. Some are holding their gloves between their teeth. Others are squeezing their morning papers under their arms, feverishly searching for change. Passenger Nyklíčková is dragging a child by its hand but its feet keep slipping. Passenger Holas angrily shakes his fist at the darkness outside.

The Seated Passengers in Transit are watching with hostility.

Driver Chodura disgustedly turns his back on the steering wheel to check the Fares being dropped into the Coinbox, which displays a multitude of no longer valid fares.

Driver Chodura closes the door, which shuts with a creak. The lights go out.

The bus starts jerkily, the Passengers grope about and tumble into its depth. The bus is moving.

Driver Chodura turns to watch the last person drop in his Fare.

DRIVER CHODURA *(huskily)*:
 From stunted forests rises whitish steam...

SEATED PASSENGERS *(in chorus, with relief)*:
 for fishermen who have run out of stream,
 for a black mirror with tenfold reflection...

PASSENGER HOLAS *(clasping a grab-hold)*:
 for empty veins of tracks and ancient highway sections...

STANDING PASSENGERS *(in chorus)*:
 for girls guarding dead geese in fields behind the byre,
 for alien plumage in fastidious fire...

Honking, the Bus brakes, Passengers not holding on lurch forward. Driver Chodura spits through his half-open window.

DRIVER CHODURA *(with gusto)*:
 Snow ripens in the fists of unborn babes...

SEATED PASSENGERS *(some of them getting up to alight, in chorus)*:
 the spider in the eye-socket begins his tales...

PASSENGER NYKLÍČKOVÁ (*pushing her way through with her child, excitedly*):
The ice tree has sprung up and towards the sky will strain…

PASSENGER HOLAS (*at the door*):
we shall not meet upon this earth again.

SEATED PASSENGERS (*in chorus*):
We shall not meet upon this earth again.

DRIVER CHODURA (*braking, the lights come on*):
We shall not meet…

SEATED PASSENGERS (*in chorus*):
…upon this earth again.

The Bus has stopped, the door opens with a hiss and suddenly there is a deep and motionless silence.

PASSENGER NYKLÍČKOVÁ'S CHILD:
We shall not meet upon this earth again.

From a great distance comes the sound of honking, but otherwise the silence is unbroken. (Nobody moves.)

[EO]

The Angel of Death

*In an indeterminate white space, which might equally be the gym of a
rehabilitational health institution as Purgatory, a double file of corpulent
citizens $C_1 - C_n$ are riding exercise bicycles from right to left; in fact they
remain stationary, pedalling. They wear white sweat-shirts and baggy
suspicious-looking track-suit trousers. The citizens do not wriggle, do not
look up, do not turn round and do not distract themselves; they just pedal
on as if the regular running of the universe depended on it.*

*Above the row of bicycles hangs a good-sized loudspeaker which opens its
black mouth and speaks in a sonorous, confidence-inspiring voice.*

LOUDSPEAKER: Such then, citizens, is the mechanism of life. The
union of sex cells is followed by explosive proliferation and differen-
tiation. From the three germ layers develop tissues and organs, and
already you have breathing, you have digestion, and little feet kick-
ing...

The citizens pedal even more zealously.

LOUDSPEAKER: ...already fluids and factors are produced, already
thinking begins, thoughts like glass fish in a black proto-sea.

*One citizen cleans his ear with his little finger and they all keep pedal-
ling.*

LOUDSPEAKER: The self is distinguished from the non-self, a boun-
dary now exists between the self and the world... The first cells
mutate and degenerate, and the life clock subtracts the first amount
from the limited number of cell divisions. Birth now takes place.
And leaving home...for schooling, training, culture. Exercise
begins, and economic activity. Unflagging enthusiasm circulates
from capillaries to the heart and back, if possible also through the
lymphatic system. One walks cheerfully down sad streets and vice
versa. One bets on the pools and new horizons open up. One makes
love. The increased level of sex hormones ruins the thymus, control
of malignant growth is reduced, malignancies occur, production of
IgG antibodies is reduced, IgM antibodies cross-react with the
body's own tissues, already we have rheumatism and collagen dis-
eases, already atherosclerotic plaques appear in the coronary
arteries, infarctions tap softly on the walls of the heart chambers...

The citizens, one after another, start pedalling at a furious rate, trying to ride away without moving from their spots.

LOUDSPEAKER: One walks sadly down sad streets, plaster falls. Even balconies fall. Maintenance has always been a problem.

Exhausted, the citizens revert to their original pace, wiping off their copious sweat in various ways.

LOUDSPEAKER: Freedom is recognised necessity. Here and there, cell division is exhausted. One is eating into one's capital. One jumps out of the way of buses. One plays the pools. Values are created. One works beyond retirement age. Culture is a function of work beyond retirement age. One turns inward. Inwardness is a function of muscular atrophies. Blood circulation is often insufficient. Especially in certain places. One embarks on a diet and on testosterone, and teeth are extracted. This is the time of wisdom and merits.

The citizens pedal on and suffer.

LOUDSPEAKER: And then, citizens, then...then comes the Angel of Death.

Darkness falls. A blood-red glow floods in from the sides. A heavy, fateful footfall is heard, rather like the monotonous sound of kettle-drums. The Angel of Death enters from the right. He is a slight little man in a rather shabby jacket and striped trousers made baggy by his knobbly knees. He has a drab briefcase and a bald head. He steps behind the last pair in such a way that none of the pedalling citizens can see him.

LOUDSPEAKER: Here's an opportunity for you, citizens. As a special treat from the management here's an opportunity for you. Speak to the Angel of Death, he's right behind you.

ANGEL OF DEATH *(suddenly yelling like a drill sergeant)*: Comrades, atten-shun! And pedal on, citizens, pedal on. Let me tell you: exercise, exercise and again exercise. Only by exercise...Call that pedalling, Olejník?...you're sitting there like a baboon on a melon ...Only by exercise do we consolidate our health...Come on, Opásek, pull those pants of yours up before they get entangled in your bloody chain...by consolidating our health and walking in the country in all weathers...Olejník, stop staring and keep pedalling ...and also by willpower do we prevent illness. And preventing illness lengthens our lives. We want a long life...Opásek, have a new elastic put in or you'll never consolidate your health that way. We want a long life so that...well, Olejník? So that...

During the last few words the Angel of Death has fished out a cigarette from his breast pocket and lit it. He now blows the smoke at citizen Olejník who is in the last pair, directly in front of him.

Citizen Olejník dismounts from his exercise bicycle and turns to the Angel of Death.

OLEJNÍK *(timidly extends his hand)*: Olejník, pleased to meet you, Mr...?

ANGEL OF DEATH: Karel Štác is my name.

They shake hands.
Citizen Olejník quietly crumples to the floor. The Angel of Death tucks his briefcase under his arm and gets on the vacant exercise bicycle.

ANGEL OF DEATH *(triumphantly)*: So that we can longer still and better still...consolidate! So that we can longer still and better still ...exercise! So we can prevent...! So we can longer still and better still...prolong! We keep pedalling and pedalling. So we can longer still and better still...

The Angel of Death chants the phrase rhythmically and the citizens adjust their pace, pedalling like a marching platoon, totally involved and with absolute confidence.

ANGEL OF DEATH *(pedalling and rhythmically chanting)*: So we can longer still and better still...so we can longer still and better still...

[EO]

Crucifix

Behind the massive Bench, at the centre, sits the Judge in a threadbare gown. On both sides of him the Assessors, made of cardboard. Below the Bench, to the right, is the dock, where the Defendant is cringing: a small bird-like man, flanked by two beefy warders. Below the Bench, on the left, is the Prosecutor, standing erect and mostly addressing the public.

Above the Judge's head is a large crucifix, with a Crucified Christ of athletic build, his loincloth more like a pair of Bermuda shorts. Christ is smoking a huge cigar, puffing at it and from time to time tapping the ash in front of the Judge or on the Judge, holding the cigar in his nail-pierced and bleeding hand.

The proceedings are well advanced.

PROSECUTOR: ...about these heinous crimes, yes, crimes, what is especially significant, yes, tremendously significant, is the defendant's pathological, though entirely conscious, and indeed calculated and calculating affection for animals. Yes, animals.

The Defendant cringes even more.

PROSECUTOR: In his flat he keeps – and this has been attested by witnesses and proved – he keeps three cats, twenty-eight mice, five of them white, one iguana and four, yes, four budgerigars. He looks after them and feeds them day and night. And this...this...person who has caused so much grief to his friends and neighbours and colleagues returns to his lair, in order to let white and grey mice out of their cages, in order to feed them on cheese, bacon, yes, and on bread and salt, and with his fingers, yes, fingers dirtied with so many machinations, to stroke the warty skin of an iguana...

The Defendant, visibly shaken, bows his head and covers his face.

PROSECUTOR: ...an iguana, in order to throw it dulled midges, yes midges, to treat it under an infra-red lamp, to fondle lazy and debauched cats and make them purr, yes, purr, while...

The Prosecutor suddenly stops as if he had forgotten his lines and lost his thread. He goes limp and looks anxious. At the same moment the Defendant abruptly stands erect. As if driven by the same mechanism the Prosecutor and the Defendant step out, in an almost ritualistic manner, and change places. The Court and the Warders do not move. The Defendant now stands in the Prosecutor's place and the Prosecutor sags and cringes between the two Warders.

DEFENDANT *(taking up naturally and without embarrassment):* ...while his colleagues and friends are collapsing under the weight of the evil done to them. Yet he cynically, yes, cynically...

The Defendant now towers high and, pointing his finger at the Prosecutor cringing between the Warders, raises his voice to a theatrical note.

DEFENDANT: ...feeds the crumbs which the mice have left to the budgerigars, giving the budgerigars sunflower seed, yes, seed, giving the budgerigars yesterday's rolls, and watches the sated love-birds preening themselves, yes, and billing and cooing. And that on a day when he had caused so much grief to his neighbours and colleagues ...first of all by...

JUDGE *(snapping out of his tense concentration, shouting):* Keep to the point, please!

The Prosecutor glances up briefly but the Defendant is thundering on:

DEFENDANT: ...Yes, to the point. On the day when so many mice go hungry, when so many cats mew hopelessly on the roofs, when so many budgerigars are threatened, yes, directly threatened by atmospheric pollution and a shortage of sunflowers, on the day when some iguanas, yes, iguanas, are literally becoming extinct, yes, physically extinct, on the day when, for instance, only two specimens of the iguana *Ophisalis corneliana* survive and, moreover, neither knows about the other!

The Defendant falls silent and looks around triumphantly. The Judge looks slowly at his watch.

JUDGE *(shouting hysterically):* Silence in Court! The case is adjourned. The Court will retire for consultation. Remain in your seats. The hearing will resume at ten o'clock.

The Judge rises. He is not very tall; his gown sits on him strangely. The Warders rise too, march up behind the Bench and grab the Judge by his shoulders. Carelessly they drag him out of the court-room. The Judge wriggles feebly in their grip.

The Prosecutor and Defendant walk up to each other, offer each other a cigarette, light up, and quietly whisper together.

Christ chucks away his cigar and spits conspicuously.

PROSECUTOR: ...No, 'is nerves ain't what they used to be. Why, under Disraeli – did ya know that? – we 'ad even trained crickets and eight squirrels.

DEFENDANT: That ain't nothing. Why, under Vespasian I even threw in a couple of young tigers.

CHRIST *(nervously)*: I say, boys, give me a hand down, will you?

The Prosecutor pulls himself out of his reverie, turns and with deliberate superiority snaps:

PROSECUTOR: You're the last straw! Just hang on up there!

[EO]

Supper à la Russell Edson

The most ordinary kitchen imaginable. A gas cooker, shelves. In the middle a table laid for a meal, its short side against the wall. At the other short side, facing the wall, sits the Child. The Mother moves from the cooker to the table with a bowl from which rises a steady cloud of steam, as from an oracle's cauldron. On the chair facing the door is a cushion and sitting on it a huge egg-shaped stone – granite, gneiss or a coping stone. Just as Mother has placed the dish on the table the door opens abruptly and Father rolls in, wearing an overcoat and scarf, and a modish hat pulled well down. At his entry the lights go up considerably and it becomes obvious that Father, Mother and the Child are wearing masks with a mildly comical grin.

FATHER: What's this then?

MOTHER: What's what? Good evening.

FATHER: What's that stone there?

MOTHER: A stone.

FATHER: Okay. What's it doing on my chair?

MOTHER: We invited it for supper.

FATHER: Who's we?

MOTHER: ...Well...we.

FATHER: Don't talk rot. Put it away. It's on my chair.

MOTHER: We invited it for supper. There's no other chair, and you weren't here.

CHILD: He's going to play with me after supper.

FATHER: Shut up! That's my place and no one's going to loll about in it. That's my place, even if I wasn't here at all. It's my place even if I spat at it only once a year. Put him away. That's my place even if I dangled from the ceiling.

MOTHER: Don't shout. We have a guest. You'll spoil his appetite.

FATHER: I didn't invite him. I didn't...Where am I to sit? What d'you suggest I do?

MOTHER: If you went past the window outside you'd be a pleasant passer-by. If you lay down by the stove you'd make a pretty pattern on the lino. If you crawled into that pot you could be a potato.

CHILD: You could sprout. I'd water you.

FATHER: Shut up! Okay. So you like that chunk of rock better than me?

MOTHER: He's... We don't like him specially at all. We just invited him for supper.

FATHER: What have you got going with him? You don't just invite...

MOTHER: There's nothing between us. He's... He just was so on his own...

FATHER: I'm on my own too.

CHILD: Go out, then... Maybe somebody'll find you.

FATHER: Shut up!

CHILD: And he's...

MOTHER: Behave yourself. You'll spoil his appetite. You'll upset his digestion. I can't stand stones with indigestion.

FATHER: I don't give a damn about what you can't stand. This is my place and this is my food.

CHILD: But he's...

MOTHER: When we've eaten you can take a bit out into the hall with you. Or to the stove. Or to the ceiling.

CHILD: But he's got a golden vein, did you know?

FATHER: ...So... Okay. So you've found a replacement for me.

MOTHER: We weren't looking for anything. You weren't looking for anything either.

CHILD: I wasn't looking for anything either.

FATHER: Shut up! Are you saying that over all these years I forgot to replace myself?

MOTHER: I'm not saying anything. I haven't been saying anything for ages. I don't know anything.

FATHER: Okay. I didn't replace myself, so you now have a replacement. I'm to lie down in the corner and wait. Okay. You're not saying anything. Okay. You don't know anything. You don't even know whose place this is or who I am.

MOTHER: I'm just dishing up the supper.

Mother lifts the lid off the dish, and even greater clouds of steam pour out, engulfing the room. With a curse Father whips off his scarf and hat, steps up to the table facing the stone and takes off his mask. He has no face: his head is made of exactly the same stone as that sitting opposite him.

Mother freezes in her movement over the dish. The Child leaps to his feet. As if on command they both take off their masks. They too, understandably, have shapeless stones instead of faces.

MOTHER *(with relief, pushing Father out of the way)*: I'm just dishing up the supper.

[EO]

Sand game

A corner of a park. Fragrant shrubs of jasmine (or mock-orange blossom). In the centre a sandpit, somewhat churned up, beyond it a spattered seat of unpainted wood. Hidden among the shrubs, but visible, is a wooden shed, into which one can see through its wrenched-off door. It contains shovels, hoes, wheel-barrows and spilled sacks of something or other.

On the seat sits a relatively young Oldster with white hair, in a leather jacket and turtleneck shirt. He is reading a newspaper which he holds permanently open in front of him, without lowering it. From time to time he peers over the top of it.

Playing in the sandpit are two relatively big children: Ilona and Robert. They have built a rather elaborate structure of sand, bits of board, wire and dogshit. It suggests a rocket launching site or the hanging gardens of Babylon.

OLDSTER *(peering over his paper)*: It says here it'll be windy with heavy showers. That'll sweep that nonsense of yours away all right!

ROBERT: That isn't actually possible. The anticyclone is still over Norway. We are still under the influence of a fairly substantial high, which is only slowly shifting to the south.

OLDSTER *(irritably)*: But that's what it says here!

ILONA: The structure is sufficiently solidly anchored. We considered all the parameters. This linkage here will stand up to a pressure of 50 grammes per square centimetre. The tolerances are considerable.

OLDSTER *(even more irritably)*: You can't make something from nothing. I don't care what tol...tol...tolerances you've got. There'll be a downpour. It says so here.

ROBERT *(adding another piece of wood)*: The information flow is often overlaid by a considerable amount of noise. It is necessary to relate the general and summary estimate to the specific system which represents only a small segment of the reality covered by the information frame. More particularly: the micro-climatic conditions of this sandpit can be defined only on the basis of physical evidence regarding the maximum number of parameters of the ambient formation.

ILONA *(adding a sand patty)*: Besides, even the essence of the artifact itself changes reality, or let us say micro-reality, to the extent that information pre-dating its creation cannot be fully valid, that is: true, after its creation.

ROBERT: This is an analogous situation to any anagenetic effect under natural conditions, which are never identical in relation to the new object, nor in relation to themselves once the object has passed from the sphere of intellectual conception to the sphere of physical realisation.

OLDSTER: You're mad. There was a blood-red sunset yesterday and the birds are flying low. It says here a bridge collapsed in Ecuador. No, wait a minute...not in Ecuador, but in what's-its-name...in Puerto Rico, no, in Malay...Malay...no, in Belgium.

ILONA *(to Robert)*: A few deep injections are needed at this point.

ROBERT *(to Ilona)*: Quite right. The added height might otherwise result in such stress that, with the given material, we might exceed the original parameters.

OLDSTER *(angrily)*: You're mad. He that mischief hatches mischief catches, don't you worry, no matter how much you...you parametrify yourself!

ROBERT *(straightening up, but with the patience typical of his age)*: In substantial thinking we certainly can relate the value of essence, or even the value of its actual statement, to a certain preformed model, with regard to which that essence of statement then appears, in some way or other, insufficient, inadequate, or indeed excessive. In such a case we may then employ verbal comparisons through which we release dissatisfaction, or frustration, caused by the immanence of the preconceived model in our thinking, no matter how we perceive it...

OLDSTER: Mad as a hatter!

ILONA: But he is, moreover, and in my opinion, rightly, a believer in non-substantial ontology...

ROBERT *(starts walking up and down and expounding in the manner of the Platonic school)*: ...because it alone enables us to free ourselves from the rigid structures of the old or new anthropological reductionism and to reconstruct our world both in terms of its phenomenology and of its freely and operationally substituted existentiality...

OLDSTER *(waving his paper)*: Oh, go to...It says here...

ROBERT *(in mounting ecstasy which causes the appearance of slight flickering and sparking around his head, eventually encircling his head as a kind of permanent greenish glow)*: ...reconstruct our world in its meaningful comprehensiveness, and that with full realisation of our involvement, and hence from within the field we are trying to comprehend, but also, up to a point, on the basis of abstraction from our own participation, on the basis of self-objectivisation and ad hoc derealisation, which of course is the beginning of genuine and permanent realisation...

OLDSTER: You're quite mad!

ROBERT *(in his ecstasy he enters the shed, complete with halo, stumbling over the junk until he is lost from sight)*: ...so that the reconstruction of the world in the system of non-substantial ontology...

From the shed comes the sound of an explosion, some pieces of timber fly out and clouds of black dirt. Ilona sits down on the sand construction and flattens it. The Oldster jumps up, shielding his head with his paper. As the noise and smoke subside a somewhat shaken Robert, now minus his halo, crawls out of the shed.

OLDSTER *(triumphantly)*: Didn't I say you were mad?

[EO]

254

Lenora

A middle-class room. Heavy, posh furniture, dominated by a secretaire-cupboard, with lots of glass and china, and a row of books. Doors on both sides. In the centre, a massive table surrounded by tall, flimsy chairs. An unseen clock ticks loudly. Enter an old man, Libor, and an old woman, Gertrude.

GERTRUDE: What time is it?

LIBOR *(without hesitation)*: Almost eight.

They scurry around like frightened mice, then sprint out, stage left. Enter from the right a girl, Lenora, and uncle Oscar, deep in a serious, evidently conspiratory dialogue. Oscar is arguing feverishly. He's dressed in the bourgeois manner, while Lenora is the one character wearing national folk-costume, with rich ornaments, frills, ribbons and leg-of-mutton sleeves.

OSCAR *(urgently)*: Now when we know where the shoe pinches...

LENORA *(in reply)*: Now when we know where the shoe pinches...

They sit down at the table, put their heads together. Lenora hesitates and withdraws slightly.

OSCAR *(more urgently – everything's at stake)*: Now when we know where the shoe pinches

    *

After a long pause, Lenora gives a deep sigh. Relieved, Oscar gets up, lifts a finger warningly, to signify the importance of the impending moment, then rushes out, stage left.

Lenora sits still while the villainous Jan creeps in from the right. He is a hunchback, dressed in tight black clothes. Mischievously, he approaches Lenora. She watches him, surreptitiously and cautiously. Jan sits down and begins to ingratiate himself with Lenora.

JAN *(sweetly)*: Now when we know where the shoe pinches...

Lenora moves away, gets up and gives another deep sigh. She walks to the cupboard, takes out a huge, blue-flowered coffee mug, and sets it in front of Jan. Jan is honoured, and cheerfully pulls his chair up to the table. Lenora exits right to fetch the coffee. Jan looks around circumspectly. Lenora returns with a pot of coffee and a sugar bowl. She steps close to Jan and adroitly pours the coffee.

LENORA *(matter-of-factly)*: Now when we know where the shoe pinches...

With the same adroitness, Lenora kicks the unoccupied chair, which crashes on its side. Jan, in a reflex action, gallantly, bends to pick it up. Instantly, Lenora takes a small folded paper out of her pocket and puts a solid dose of poison into the coffee. She produces a spoon from her other pocket and hands it to Jan.

Jan sits down, stirs the coffee and mumbles.

JAN: Now when we know where the shoe pinches...

Jan doesn't like the coffee, smells it and turns to Lenora. She looks away. Jan takes another sip.

Suddenly, a sweet playful song sounds from the left. It is sung by a delightful tenor, with extraordinary charm and intensity. Lenora straightens up and listens. She cannot resist, and cries out merrily.

LENORA: Now when we know where the shoe pinches...

Jan jumps up and runs to the cupboard, pulls out a rifle and some ammunition from behind the dishes, and runs to the door, loading. But he begins to wobble.

JAN *(raucously)*: Now when we know where the shoe pinches...

Exit Jan. Stamping feet are heard from both wings.

TENOR *(offstage, exclaiming)*: Now when we know where the shoe pinches...

A loud shot and a falling body are heard.

LENORA *(crossing herself)*: Now when we know where the shoe pinches...

Lenora sits down in front of the table, centre. Her body is stiff. All of a sudden, the room becomes very dark.

Libor and Gertrude enter from the right and trudge in front of Lenora without noticing anything.

GERTRUDE: What time is it?

LIBOR: Almost eight.

They trot around and sprint out, stage right.

A number of plain-clothes policemen, attracted by the shot, suddenly rush into the room through both doors. They all look the same, like peas in a pod; all wear mackintoshes and caps. They snoop around, open the cupboard, crawl under the table and dash at Lenora, tearing off her ribbons and frills. They scrutinise them thoroughly and put them into boxes.

Two policemen enter, bringing Libor and Gertrude. From the right, Jan creeps in and flops under the cupboard. Nobody pays any attention.

The police sergeant (mackintosh and cap) switches on a bright light. He turns out to be Oscar. He walks to Lenora and turns on a large floor lamp, turning it to her face. Lenora is stubbornly silent. The policeman shakes her ruthlessly and bangs on the table.

LENORA *(scared to death)*: Now when we know where the shoe pinches...

The sergeant writes the words down in a notebook, nodding, quite satisfied.

The policemen are getting ready to leave when the sergeant sees Libor and Gertrude. He gives a signal, two policemen hold them, and he directs the lamp at their faces.

The sergeant stamps his foot.

SERGEANT: What time is it?

LIBOR: I don't know.

[DY/DH]

Door II

Antechamber of an historical event. Heavy brocade curtains. In the middle a massive door leading into there. Above it, a coat of arms, ancient handiwork. In the corner, a solid table and chairs with pompous backs. In front, a pendulum clock, larger than life, ticking relentlessly. It strikes every two minutes, producing a dulcet sound.

Enter Fibbersoldier, investigates the room, listens at the curtain right, at the door, at the curtain left, circumspectly examines the pendulum clock and sets his own pocket pendulum clock accordingly. After which he circumspectly hides behind the pendulum clock.

Enter Captain (beard, pistol) and two soldiers (short swords and notebooks in hand).

CAPTAIN: Come here, Weissberger! Come here, Maximovich!

Soldiers slouch around, shuffling in various directions, more away from than toward the Captain.

CAPTAIN: Well! The decisive moment is near. The greatest caution! caution! is imperative. Everything depends on the three of us! *(Louder)* We have to speak in a low voice. Are we alone?

SOLDIER WEISSBERGER *(shouts)*: We are!

The soldiers stop as far as possible from the Captain. Fibbersoldier lurks and listens. Now and then he writes a note on his cuff.

CAPTAIN: You, Weissberger, get ready at the door!

Weissberger sits comfortably at the table and throws his tools under the chair.

CAPTAIN: You, Maximovich, will knock!

Maximovich sits at the table and props his feet up.

CAPTAIN *(with growing élan, moving down stage)*: You will enter and find out if he is asleep!

SOLDIER MAXIMOVICH *(behind the table, after a long pause)*: He's sleeping like a log.

CAPTAIN: Good! Find out if he's alone!

MAXIMOVICH *(behind the table, after a very long pause)*: He is.

CAPTAIN: This job is a piece of cake.

He rubs his hands. He sits at the table and takes out a flask, pours himself a gobletful, and drinks it. He offers the flask to the soldiers, who gratefully but lazily take swigs. Fibbersoldier creeps from his hiding place and takes out a goblet, into which he slyly puts a few drops of poison. He hands it to the Captain, who pours. Fibbersoldier hurriedly drinks and hides.

CAPTAIN: Draw!

Soldiers sit. Fibbersoldier lurks.

CAPTAIN: Jump and stab!

Soldiers sit.

CAPTAIN *(with great enthusiasm)*: History is...uh what's...is watching you!

Soldiers sit.

CAPTAIN *(excited, pours)*: Stab above the fourth rib, three fingers from the chestbone. Three fingers!

Maximovich drinks and raises his hand with three fingers up. He scrutinises his fingers with pleasure.

CAPTAIN: And stab above the third rib too! One never knows!

Soldiers sit and drink. Captain pours diligently.

CAPTAIN: Weissberger, follow Maximovich!

Soldiers sit.

CAPTAIN *(pours again)*: Search the boxes! Take out the papers! Don't step in anything!

Soldiers sit.

CAPTAIN *(gulps down a gobletful)*: Have you got it?

Soldiers sit and stare.

CAPTAIN *(thrilled)*: Have you got it?

WEISSBERGER *(jerks, after a thoughtful deliberation)*: Yep.

CAPTAIN: Splendid! Excellent! The homeland will...will...always remember you...or something. Haven't you stepped in anything?

Soldier W. falls asleep. Soldier M. slumbers, dreamily caressing the leg of the chair with his finger.

CAPTAIN: Cover all the traces! No one must find them. Secrecy and super-secrecy! Stratagems and super-stratagems!

Fibbersoldier crawls from behind the clock, pours himself some poison, taps the Captain's shoulder and hands him the goblet. Captain hurriedly pours.

FIBBERSOLDIER *(lugubriously)*: Thanks.

CAPTAIN: You're welcome.

Fibbersoldier hides again, drinking. Soldiers sit and doze.

CAPTAIN: And now, retreat! Weissberger to the right, Maximovich to the left! I will send a report to the legate! Hurry! Eye for eye! Death for death! Measure for measure!

Everybody sits contentedly.

CAPTAIN *(with maximum effort and enthusiasm)*: Everything depends on accuracy. Everything depends on speed. The children will...will ...learn about it...I think! Let us go! We are flying! We have won! For the legate! For the homeland! For lawfulness! For...*(he doesn't know, waves his hand).*

Everybody sits on. The clock strikes. All of a sudden the door creaks slightly and in the absolute silence begins to open; it is wide open and gapes. It leads into boundless darkness.

Fibbersoldier, lurking behind the clock, and the Captain notice it, watch with interest, but do not move. The soldiers sit and doze.

A soft, plaintive sound is suddenly heard from beyond the door; it gathers momentum, turning into tiny shrieks, barking, whining, lamenting and culminating in an inhuman, quivering howl.

[DY/DH]

260

Questioning

The greasy spoon Aurora. At the table moribund eaters and drinkers hunch over their plates, beer glasses and cups. At the hot food counter a solitary employee counts bills, which is obviously too much for him. There is an exit from the street, but no other door, because elderliness is not something anybody can pass through. Enter the middle-aged Questioner, dislocated in time and space. He hovers near the hot food counter for a while, but fails to excite the counting employee's interest. Consequently, he turns to the table of Beer Drinkers.

QUESTIONER *(timidly)*: Excuse me please, can you tell me how to get to the pet store that sells birds?

FIRST BEER DRINKER *(slightly intoxicated)*: Whaddya need birds for, buddy?

In the ensuing silence only the scratching of cutlery in the gravy is heard.

SECOND BEER DRINKER: I knew a guy who had a cricket in a cage. It was some imported cricket.

FIRST BEER DRINKER: Did it make any noise?

SECOND BEER DRINKER: I guess it did. But in fact it was a stiff.

FIRST BEER DRINKER: Well, a cricket won't last, imported or not imported.

SECOND BEER DRINKER: A bird won't last long either. I knew a guy...

The Questioner tries to attract attention.

SECOND BEER DRINKER *(quickly)*: ...he used to buy stuff in that store. It's...it's round the corner...on the way to...what's its name ...to Mělník.

FIRST BEER DRINKER: You crazy or something? It's round the third corner, like you go to the first traffic light and turn uphill, left, you see a sign saying Linen, but they sell surplus vegetables from co-ops, but most of the time the joint is closed.

SECOND BEER DRINKER: Well, you got it all wrong. For sure. It's round the corner, then you go downhill, first uphill, see, and then down, that's the place where old Vokáč slipped and fell on Abrham's car and Abrham was just starting the car and he got such a scare he backed the car up and knocked over that vegetable-seller's stand

...but then he went forward and ran into that old bag's cart, the cart got going and they found it down at the reservoir...The vegetable guy ran out and cursed the broad, and she snapped at Abrham, and Abrham was so rattled he forgot to step on the brakes and crashed into some garbage cans. Old Vokáč was run over by somebody anyway, but no one knew if by Abrham or that cart or that guy who was driving by and stopped to help them...Then they all put the blame on that old bag, but she wasn't in her right mind so they didn't get anything from her. So that's where it is, your store, where that cart passed.

The Questioner starts to retreat, but is stopped.

FIRST BEER DRINKER: You couldn't be more wrong, pal. That happened somewhere else, because Vokáč went home from the On the Corner pub, and everybody in there heard it and went looking for that cart, because that woman had got lost. What pet store! That store is near the place where that blonde broad used to live, that dame who had five kids and two daddies for each of them, ten altogether, so that each kid has a different family name, but also a different one from the daddies' names because they could never make up their mind about it, and she kept forgetting them. So the kids, they called each other by their family names, because all the boys were Peters and both girls were Marys. That blonde dame could never think of any other name when she got knocked up... So the kids used to hang around at the store window looking at them birds and monkeys, and they'd say, see Novák, I'd like that parrot, and Novák said, no way, Lederer, I want that monkey, right, Strnišková? So you see, it's round the third corner on the left, where that blonde piece used to live.

During the discourse on the blonde, eaters at the next table become interested, and an old woman with a tablespoon shuffles near from her finished soup.

SOUP WOMAN: Well, pardon me, I'm sure, but that blonde dame lives at the water reservoir, where they had that fire so many times... and she's got eight kids and they *(flourishing her spoon like a rapier)* ...they once almost burned down that green house, playing firemen, and that green house belonged to old Němcová, she kept writing letters to her stepson in the army, he'd written her twice that he was killed in action, but he wasn't, he just wanted to get rid of her, but she just kept writing and only stopped when someone told her there was no war...so she started fixing up the place, thinking her son was coming back, and she put some old junk in the hall, and the blonde dame's kids played there and almost set the house on fire, but the stuff didn't burn too well...

The Questioner makes an attempt to withdraw, but the Meat Eater approaching from the next table stops him.

MEAT EATER *(clutching the Questioner's sleeve, as if intending to drag him to the witness box)*: I don't know what you're talking about, but you could see that fire from as far as Vysočany, and it all happened two blocks from here... And it was no kids who did it, it was spontaneous combustion. Spontaneous combustion is a special chemical process of unknown origin and I've found out...

Annoyance and grumbling flare up among the Beer Drinkers.

MEAT EATER *(with increased effort)*: ...and it is provoked by the contact of two substances, for instance a hard and a soft substance, which makes the soft substance thicken and smoulder, while the hard substance...

FIRST BEER DRINKER: Stuff it, where do ya get soft stuff in hay?

MEAT EATER *(ignoring him)*: For instance, spontaneous combustion in writings bound in cloth or leather, while in stitched books...

SECOND BEER DRINKER: Yeah, but they gotta be rotten inside and you gotta have 'em near a stove.

MEAT EATER: Oh yes, I mean no, my *Health Guide* once caught fire and it spread to *The Classic Legends of Antiquity*...

The Beer Drinkers try to stop him and tug at the Questioner's clothes, as if it were all his fault, while the spoon-fencing Soup Woman grabs the floor:

SOUP WOMAN: You see, a fire, it's your destiny. If you are an Aries or a Cancer, and you got white spiders at home...

MEAT EATER: ...and it also occurs when a dull and a smart material get in touch...

FIRST BEER DRINKER: Yeah, Abrham once went from the Bistro...

SOUP WOMAN: ...and white spiders make white webs, and if they get into somebody's home, the person will die of fever or fire from those white webs...

MEAT EATER: ...for instance, one Sunday afternoon, Stendhal...

FIRST BEER DRINKER: ...and Vokáč got run over for the second time...

SOUP WOMAN: ...They don't see them white spiders and think they got black ones, but the fire is already on the roof...

SECOND BEER DRINKER: They got a fine mess at home!

MEAT EATER: ...and therefore, he keeps his slim volumes of poetry...

They all flock together, shouting and waving their arms. The Questioner disappears in the sudden commotion.

SOUP WOMAN *(shrieks)*: ...and those who have white webs in their hair...

FIRST BEER DRINKER: And Vokáč got up and he says to the kid, Novák, where's that monkey...

SOUP WOMAN: ...and whoever kills a white spider is sure to drown, like that old Němcová, when she fixed up her place...

MEAT EATER: Because poetry also begins when dull and smart matters touch, tough and soft...

SECOND BEER DRINKER: And Vokáč wrote on the wall: There's no Abrham // Abrham is gone!

SOUP WOMAN: ...People don't know they have webs and no hair... But the webs keep catching and catching...

FIRST BEER DRINKER: Abrham said he couldn't run him over...

SOUP WOMAN: And the spiders were waiting and waiting...

Suddenly they all fall silent, because a skylark flies up above the counting employee, flutters below the ceiling, followed by their eyes, and sings as if a ploughman walked happily through his field. A cricket can be heard between the skylark's trilling notes. From the back emerges a king-size bird dressed in a hat and overcoat, and walks hesitantly among the tables.

FIRST BEER DRINKER *(matter-of-factly)*: Get a load of this! Must be some loony in that crazy outfit. What were we talking about?

[DY/DH]

Fairy tales

A room in a cottage, cosy and warm. Real sweet home. In the corner, an old-fashioned stove. On the walls hang ancestral portraits, saints and statesmen, shelves with particularly big tins with spices, among which bay leaves look most prominent. There is no table. The stove faces a large window, strangely bare. Right under it is a stool with Granny on it, and other stools around with a finite number of children. Only the lamp at the stove is lit. It is almost dark, and the clear window seems to let in a strong night light.

GRANNY *(with traditional kindness)*: Once upon a time. In a green castle above the black forest lived a king and he had three daughters. But he was not a good king. He spoiled the ship for a ha'porth of tar, and there wasn't enough food to lure a mouse from a hole. The king was lantern-jawed, hatchet-faced and spindle-shanked. The princesses were always poorly. They had no servants and had to make two bites of a cherry left from breakfast last for lunch. Things went from bad to worse and they literally lived on air...

While Granny is speaking, a man in a leather coat and beret slowly emerges behind her back and presses his face against the window. The gleaming eyes stare inside, grow brighter, glow and glare. Hands with fingers spread to touch the glass. When the figure has covered the whole window it suddenly disappears, probably stabbed or shot.

GRANNY *(slightly halting)*: ...that they literally lived on air, so the king called his three daughters together and said...

An enormous rooster's head turns up behind the window, opening its beak. A clawed paw pushes forward and tears it down. Feathers swirl as if a flock of ravens has landed.

GRANNY: ...and he said: Dear daughters, I don't know what to do! I'll soon be pushing up daisies, and if this goes on, you won't get married till the cows come home. You have to wander in the world a bit. First...

Feathers swirl and a beautiful naked girl or something similar appears. She clutches at the window, but a bull's head rises behind her and black hairy hands seize her breasts and pull her down. A distant sound of broken glass is heard, long echoing in gusts of wind.

GRANNY *(speaking louder)*: First you, Annie. Take that dress out of the wardrobe, so you don't look like Job's turkey...

265

In a chaotic confusion, heads of cyclopes rush to the window, heads full of teeth, heads full of snakes, sticks full of eyes, trees full of legs, hands, hooves and stumps, and they soundlessly try to break in.

GRANNY: ...go through the black forest...

Shadows of ghosts spill in, flutter through the room and cover everything.

GRANNY: ...when you come to the village, knock at the door of the first cottage.

Like a shot, everything disappears, but the window and the wall split in the middle and frosty white light flows in. From the distance, two men in coats and berets approach with terrifying ease, spreading a black, growing cape. The cape covers more and more space with an impermeable black shade.

GRANNY: ...when Johnny opens the door, tell him...

The music grows louder and fills the space. Then, in double-quick time, everything is as before. The window with the strong light, walls, the room, cosy and warm, portraits, tins with spices. Children on stools. But there is no Granny. Only the empty white stool. However, as before Granny's voice goes on:

VOICE FROM THE EMPTY STOOL: Once upon a time. In a green castle above the black forest lived a king and he had three daughters. But he was not a good king. He spoiled the ship for a ha'porth of tar, and there wasn't enough food to lure a mouse from a hole. The king was lantern-jawed, hatchet-faced and spindle-shanked.

One of the children, who have so far been quiet and immobile, turns to another.

CHILD *(with a cheerful gesture)*: I dig it, don't you?

[DY/DH]

Super-Aesop

For the combat with the birds the lion summoned all quadruped beasts. On the appointed day all were assembled. Even the donkey and the hare were present.

'Come, come,' mumbled the bear, and the wolf and tiger laughed, 'what on earth do we need these scary, good-for-nothing dolts for? Let them clear out!'

'You're wrong there,' declared the wiser lion. 'They may not be good fighters, but the donkey will be a fine trumpeter and the hare will make a speedy envoy.'

At that moment all the beasts gathered at the entrance of the Czech Nationalist Museum, where they were welcomed by Václav Rodomil Kramerius,* dressed in a morning suit.

And the lion in his wise deliberation already has shown himself to be prudent above all others.

From the underground station the hare comes up and announces that unknown but handsome beasts are approaching. The donkey trumpets a welcome and the quintruped beasts, Detmolt and Milétek, step forth draped in a kind of metal attire and with elongated intelligencer tentacles on the head. (Here we have in mind Czech nationalist science fiction of the time.) And these particular beasts have just arrived at the Vltava underground station by space-ship from the planet Sirius.

LION: Hail and welcome!

DETMOLT *(cheerfully waving his tentacles)*: Greetings, and whatever has brought you all down here on the steps?

LION *(with sudden gravity)*: A battle with the birds is in preparation, a fierce battle, for which we are now trying to work out a well-designed plan.

BEAR *(who belongs to the General Staff and hence always extracts some instruction or significance from speeches)*: Come, come.

MILÉTEK *(scratching a tentacle with his fifth leg: he is equally of gentle and feeble mind)*: And what for?

---

* Václav Rodomil Kramerius (1792-1861) was a widely known patriotic Czech journalist and publicist, and publisher of a nationalist newspaper. He translated Aesop's fables, much in vogue at the time. The first three paragraphs above are taken directly from one fable rendering.

TIGER : 'Cos the birds have become a pack of scoundrels and raise themselves on their wings above all of us beasts.

SKUNK: And that, by God, we will never put up with.

All the beasts growl consent, the donkey trumpets.

WOLF *(as soon as there is silence)*: They float in the air, but come down and squat on the ground, yes, and foul it!

TIGER: They claim lots for their nests!

DORMOUSE: They gobble the fruit and the fruit-bearers too!

DONKEY: They caw!

OX: Cackle!

SKUNK: They stink and so bring on storms.

HARE: They have a cloaca instead of... They're stupid trash.

LION *(closing the discussion in a principled way)*: They're a Tertiary mistake.

BEAR: So, so.

DETMOLT *(swaying his tentacles and gropacles searchingly)*: And in what manner do you propose to wage this battle?

OX: By hooves.

LION: Talons and teeth.

SKUNK: Stink.

TIGER: Tearing and tugging.

DONKEY: Up hill and down dale.

HARE: Indiscriminately.

BEAR: By the general prohibition of flying.

FOX: By the exhaustion of air and clouds.

WOLF: By the abolition of height.

LION: By the absolute unity of words and deeds.

DETMOLT: I just don't get it. I've a better idea.

LION: Ah, ha! Speak up, stranger.

The beasts crowd together, hanging upon the polyethylene rim of his oral cavity.

DETMOLT: This Milétek here, when he gets an idea or something crosses his mind, he straightaway acts on it. Unfortunately, he hardly ever thinks at all. But his potential may have a different result. Whenever Milétek refuses to allow something to enter his head, it just ceases to exist, right at that moment.

LION *(royally)*: Ah, yes.

TIGER *(also flummoxed)*: Whew!

DETMOLT: So if we trick Milétek into thinking that the cuckoo doesn't exist, he's going to believe it, and that'll be finis for the cuckoo.

FOX: So it won't cuckoo.

DETMOLT: Not just that. The main thing, which necessarily follows, is that the cuckoo will be victoriously finished off.

LION *(royally)*: And that's the thing. That would be excellent.

DETMOLT: I agree. But let's make a little experiment right away. A museum is a place where birds are generally exhibited, is it not?

OX: Yes, it is. Let's go then.

All the beasts press towards the main entrance, where they form themselves into the customary queue, which is so long it can't be surveyed. Václav Rodomil Kramerius slips into the box-office and hands out admission tickets, which he immediately collects and tucks in his morning suit pocket. Detmolt and Milétek are admitted without ceremony, for Milétek swallowed his ticket upon receipt.

Finally the head of the procession, including the lion, bear and both cosmonaut beasts, enter the exhibition room of predatory birds. The air smells of napthalene. On the floor an egg is rolling.

BEAR: Lo and behold, 'n eagle.

DETMOLT: What shall we begin with?

LION: It's all the same. Let's say with the eagle.

MILÉTEK *(prancing about and clapping his tentacles)*: Not a jot of 'n eagle – I've been saying it for donkey's years. *(Sits down on the floor and makes notes in a white note-book which he takes from his armour. Clearly it's the red book of the species under threat of extinction.)*

Silence. All hold their breath. The ox's belly rumbles.

Clicking is heard in the eagles' display case. Simultaneously on all identification labels the word Eagle disappears. All that remains is: Rock, Royal, Smallest, Decoy, Screeching, Sea, Bearded Vulture.

The egg stops rolling and becomes transparent. It is empty. The stuffed eagles become ashen, turn white, merge with their background, and in the end remain only in outline. Their outlines are sitting not sitting upon a nest or branch, they grip do not grip their prey their non-prey, they hang do not hang from the wire non-wire with opened wings. They are erased and have no names.

DETMOLT : And what are they?

MILÉTEK: Who?

(An awkward, stiff pause.)

FOX *(first to recover)*: And now there's room for little foxes.

OX: And now there's room for calves.

DORMOUSE: And now there's room for little dormice.

SKUNK: So the calves are going to sit on a branch?

OX *(inspired to prophecy)*: And it shall come to pass that there shall be a new generation of tree calves...And there shall be a new breed of cattle, and of swine...

BEAR: Come, come, better think it over!

MILÉTEK *(encouraged by the general exaltation)*: There aren't any cuckoos, not a trace. I've been saying it for donkey's years. *(Sits on the floor and makes notes.)*

Clicking is heard from the next room. The hare runs up to report.

HARE: There are no cuckoos, neither in the eggs nor on the labels.

The donkey trumpets.

LYNX *(renowned for his zoo-philosophical studies, raises himself up on the branch in the show-case, and holds forth)*: By this act of non-objectivist ontology our knowledge is liberated from the pernicious bonds of Cartesianism. Because all true knowledge reveals itself solely as incarnate or physical; and thus is at every point incomplete and comprehensible only by overall perception, not merely by rational abstraction. As Merleau-Ponty says, physical knowledge is lateral knowledge, as distinct from vertical, which is derived from the mind's elevation of itself above the body. As a consequence the birds, by means of their airborneness and verticality, sought to avoid lateral or co-existential knowledge, and yes, even shunned it and looked down on Nature with an immanent feeling of superiority, so doing by their way of thinking which from such a height made Nature appear merely as object, in no way, however, as interlocutor or friendly associate. While being the apparent masters of earthly objects, in their behaviour, restricted by their species, genus and family, they concurrently lost touch with the world and reached the state of complete de-zoologisation. Such being the case, they are revealed as a Cartesian disease of the planet. By means of Milétek's act, or decarnation, they have been allocated an ontologically appropriate position.

270

BEAR *(tapping the case)*: There, there.

WOLF *(shedding his fur)*: This is giving me goose-flesh all over.

MILÉTEK *(grasping his opportunity)*: There aren't any geese, not even a trace of 'em. I've always said so! *(Quickly notes it down, standing.)*

The wolf temporarily disappears, but soon regains colour, though quite flabbergasted.

FOX *(poking him)*: You're gaping like a silly…!

LION *(rounding off appreciatively the lynx's homily)*: In a word, the birds are going to get it in the neck.

BAT *(trying more and more to hide in the bear's fur)*: Just let's hope that these cosmonaut chaps won't make a mistake!

FOX: Don't be a silly sw…Of course these cosmonauts here also fly. There's honour among crows…

MILÉTEK *(romping around, fanning himself with his gropacles)*: There are no swans. No crows, no ravens, haha…

Throughout the museum there is the sound of constant clicking. The hare runs off, hardly catching breath.

HARE: There are no swans on the labels, the hahas aren't in their nests, the crows aren't on their wires, the ravens aren't anywhere…

FOX *(quickly correcting himself)*: …and there's honour among others too.

LION *(roaring amidst the general excitement)*: Hurrah for practice! Victory will be ours! Long live beasts and cosmonauts! God willing, it shall not be that Cartesians…, that cloacae…

DETMOLT: And which will?

MILÉTEK: Who will?

Beasts and cosmonauts file out of the museum to the thunderous chanting of the martial song: 'When all the world is young, lad, / And all the trees are green; / And every…a…, lad, / And every lass a queen.' Mingling with the words of the song comes the squeaking of Milétek: 'There are no geese, no nightingales, no golden nightingales, no boots, no horses…'

The donkey trumpets.

At the rear only the bear remains with Detmolt.

BEAR *(bending over Detmolt's electronic sensor in the subsiding uproar)*: Look here, couldn't you drop him a hint about the lion? You know,

271

the lion – but you can't know it – the lion in Venice always had wings...And the sphinx had wings – and the griffin had wings and it was a regular bird. And all of 'em were lions...There you have it...What about it?

When they also leave, Václav Rodomil Kramerius comes forward and declaims: 'Where angels fear to tread, cosmonauts rush in. Such we may say is the significance of this science fantasy story.'

[IM/JM]

Miroslav Holub was born in Pilsen, Czechoslovakia, in 1923. His father was a lawyer for the railways, his mother a language teacher. In 1942 he was conscripted to work on the railways. After the war he studied medicine at Charles University in Prague. He did not write poetry at all until he started clinical research at the age of thirty. He is now chief research immunologist at the Institute of Clinical and Experimental Medicine in Prague.

His Czech publications include 14 books of poetry and 5 books of essays or sketches. He has also published many learned papers on immunology. His scientific publications include the monograph *Immunology of Nude Mice* (CRC Press, Boca Raton, Florida, 1989); his essays on science and culture are collected in *The Dimension of the Present Moment* (Faber & Faber, 1990).

He writes a popular, wittily idiosyncratic newspaper column, and published these "column articles" or mini essays (subtitled *Notes and objections, maximum length 43 lines*) in 1987 as *K principu rolničky*. An English edition of this book, *The Jingle Bell Principle* translated by James Naughton, is published by Bloodaxe Books in 1990.

Holub was first introduced to English readers in 1967 when Penguin published his *Selected Poems* in their Modern European Poets series, with translations by George Theiner and Ian Milner. His next two books were translated by Ian and Jarmila Milner: *Although* (Jonathan Cape, 1971) and *Notes of a Clay Pigeon* (Secker & Warburg, 1977). In America two volumes of his poetry appeared in Oberlin's Field Translation Series: *Sagittal Section: Poems New and Selected*, translated by Stuart Friebert and Dana Hábová. By this time his work was widely published in translation in English and other languages, but it was not being published in Czechoslovakia, where his name had appeared on a government list, 'not for a poem, not for a book' but for signing a petition in the street. One of his poetry books was banned, others just not published; when his first book for over ten years appeared in a small edition in 1982, it sold out in a day, but could not be reprinted 'due to the paper shortage'.

In 1984 Bloodaxe Books published a selection of his poetry from the 1970s and 1980s, *On the Contrary and other poems*, translated by Ewald Osers. This brought together the poems of *Naopak*, which had been published in Prague in 1982, and a new collection, *Interferon, or On Theatre*, which was not published in Czechoslovakia until 1986, although parts of it were read or performed on stage in 1984 at Prague's Viola Poetry Theatre. Holub's poems from the 1950s and 1960s were collected in *The Fly* (Bloodaxe Books, 1987), translated by Ian & Jarmila Milner, Ewald Osers and George Theiner.

His latest collection of poems is *Vanishing Lung Syndrome*, translated by David Young (Faber & Faber, 1990).

Miroslav Holub's *Poems Before & After: Collected English Translations* (Bloodaxe Books, 1990) brings together all the poems from *The Fly* and *On the Contrary*, with some additional translations. It was to have been published in this form in 1984, but the Czech authorities would not allow Holub to publish a Collected Poems in Britain. He was not a member of the Czech Writers Union, and a Collected Poems was an honour reserved for only their most distinguished writers. The book was therefore published in two halves: the second half first in 1984, and the first half second in 1987.